HOPE

IS WHERE THE
HEART IS

HOPE
IS WHERE THE
HEART IS

A STORY OF A
MARRIAGE BROKEN
AND RESTORED

JIM POURTEAU

with Shannon Pourteau *and* Ken Abraham

Foreword by Dr. Joe Beam

Forefront
BOOKS

Published by Forefront Books.

Print ISBN: 978-1-63763-105-8
E-book ISBN: 978-1-63763-106-5

Cover Design by Bruce Gore, Gore Studio, Inc.
Interior Design by PerfecType, Nashville, TN

LCCN: 2022910860

For my wife, Shannon.

Your acceptance, grace, vision, and commitment have given me the faith to believe in myself, our relationship, and that miracles do happen! The strength and love you demonstrate every day is without description. Thank you for being the hands and heart of God in my life—and my hero.

CONTENTS

ACKNOWLEDGMENTS

Rob Beckham. You've believed in me from day one! You're my manager, but more than that, you are my best friend and confidant. We are going to help people live better lives—abundant ones!

Dr. Joe Beam. You were the first person who had faith in my restoration and recovery as a leader and speaker, so much so, you made me an integral part of your work. You invested your knowledge and wisdom in me. None of this exists today if you had not believed in me that Sunday night.

My father, Jim Pourteau, who taught me that giving is more about who I am and what's in my heart than what people deserve.

My stepmother, Karen Pourteau, who is the human example of love, grace, and care and has been a rock for our family.

My mother, whom I love and who is an example of perseverance. You sacrificed more than anyone could know for Marcus and me, and I am grateful for that.

PawPaw and Gagee. Y'all have always been my example of how I want my marriage to be. I miss you more than I can articulate, but your legacy continues in us.

Ken Abraham. Writing this book with you has been an amazing experience! You really are the best of the best! You were able to take hours of conversations and bring it all together to become *hope*.

Jonathan Merkh and Forefront Books. Thank you for believing in the story and jumping on board from the start.

Jen Lackey. Managing me is an impossible task! Yet you have stepped up to the plate every single day and have led this huge team in meeting deadlines and downright getting it done! Thank you for your hard work and friendship.

To you, those who wake every day and decide, "I will. Go on . . . I will believe!" You are the true Champions of Hope! May your heart receive the gift of Hope as you read these pages.

FOREWORD

This book will change you—unless you're perfect.

It's the story of pain hiding inside a dazzling personality. The story of a man overflowing with confidence and charm that draw people to him, yet a man who has far too often been afraid to be alone with himself.

Ultimately, it is a story of victory. Not the "happily ever after" fantasy in fairy tales, but a victory of healing and hope—and an amazing future.

Jim Pourteau walked into one of our "Marriages in Crisis" intensive workshops a few years back. His wife, Shannon, had found us and asked him to attend. Their marriage was in serious trouble. Jim had ripped their life apart.

I thought we were meeting Jim at the lowest point of his life.

Not so. Not by a long shot.

I've occasionally wondered if Satan ever notices a supremely gifted child and decides, *No, can't ignore this one. They'll be a powerful force against us. Let's start destroying this kid's life as quickly as possible.* If so, Jim is the poster child.

The more our friendship developed over the years, the deeper Jim revealed himself, the rejections that shaped him, and the people who used him. If it takes experiencing deep pain to ever comprehend pure joy, Jim knows a level of joy most of us never will.

Read his story in these pages. Sometimes you'll think *That's me! Wow, that's why I react like that.* Other times you'll think, *Is that me? Is Jim's story giving me insight into myself?*

Beyond this gripping story, you'll learn some of the key principles we teach to people in relationship crisis. You'll find yourself changed in very good ways.

Jim and Shannon speak transparently throughout the book. It's not a typical marriage book, and it certainly isn't a typical *Christian* marriage book. It's real life and real people serving a real God.

If you are ready to be real, turn the page.

Dr. Joe Beam
Marriage Helper

A NOTE FROM THE AUTHOR

Perspective matters. People may experience the same events yet perceive them in totally different ways. The stories within these pages are written from my perspective and based on my recollections. Other individuals who witnessed these same events may have divergent opinions or remember matters differently, but this book reflects my experiences and contains my perceptions of them. I have combined or compressed certain events and taken some artistic license in recreating conversations. In some instances, I have created composites and, in others, changed individual's names and details. My wife, Shannon, has read every word and concurs with the accuracy of the stories I have shared. We hope you benefit from the truths we have learned.

—Jim Pourteau

PART I

LOOKING FOR THE RIGHT ROAD

I Love You, but I'm Not in Love with You

I never thought the words would emerge from my mouth. I'd heard countless husbands and wives say something similar about their spouses, but I never dreamed that I might feel the same way about my wife, Shannon. We had been high school sweethearts and had dated for more than four years prior to getting married. But now, after nearly twenty years of marriage, I couldn't get away from those thoughts and words. I knew what I had to express to Shannon: "I love you, but I don't love you the way a husband should love his wife."

They were complicated words. After all, I was the go-to guy who did and said everything "right" when other people needed advice about doing the right thing. I was a spiritual leader and a pastor in one of the largest congregations in the Northeast.

And I was having sex with one of my wife's best friends.

One day in early autumn of 2010, Shannon and I were in our beautifully furnished formal living room in our recently built home in Massachusetts. As kids who had both come from divorced families, we grew up poor. When Shannon and I married, our first home cost us a whopping $1,000. Now, twenty years later, we felt as though we were living in luxury—and by our standards, we were. It was everything we had ever wanted. But it was an emotional prison of gold. A lovely home and elegant drapes and furniture cannot satisfy a lonely, emotionally disconnected heart.

Shannon was sitting in a chair when I walked in, and without giving her any warning, I said, "I don't love you anymore. I'm ready to give up everything—you, this house; I'm willing to walk away from twenty years of ministry. I'm in love with someone else."

Shannon looked up at me, shocked. "What?"

I stared directly at Shannon and said the words I had been thinking for months. "I love you," I said, "but I don't love you like a husband should."

"I don't understand," Shannon protested. "How can you say that?"

"I think I love someone else . . . and not you," I admitted. Then I said it again, as if to drive home the point. "I love you, but I don't love you the way a husband should love his wife."

My words had taken Shannon completely by surprise. She might have suspected that something was causing me to be disgruntled, like a midlife crisis or maybe too much stress at work, but had anyone asked her five minutes earlier about the status of our marriage, Shannon would have sung my praises. She was happy and contented with our life together.

She remained seated in the chair. I continued standing in front of her, making no effort to console her. She was fighting back tears, trying hard not to cry, but she was losing that battle.

"Don't do anything yet. Just relax," she said softly. "Jimmy, what are you talking about? Every single day for the past twenty years, you've told me you love me . . . and now *this*? I don't understand."

Shannon's body sank more deeply into the chair. Her big brown eyes glistened, not with the excitement or joy that I had seen for years, but with huge tears welling up in them. I had looked into those beautiful eyes for comfort, faith, and assurance, but now all I could see there was pain.

The hurt look in Shannon's eyes saddened me. I immediately looked away and steeled myself, including my own facial expression and demeanor. I couldn't allow her pain to penetrate my heart. I didn't want to deviate from my decision. I was in love with another woman, and I knew what I wanted—or so I thought.

I left the room, and for several hours we didn't speak. Later that day, Shannon and I drove from Shrewsbury, Massachusetts, to Boston—about a thirty-mile jaunt east on Interstate 90—to attend a wedding reception held aboard a boat in Boston Harbor. Most of the people who had been invited were from our church, and I was their pastor.

While driving, I kept telling Shannon, "I just don't love you as I should."

She didn't reply. She sat calmly, looking out the window and not responding positively or negatively. Eventually, she spoke quietly, as though talking to herself as much as to me. "That can't be," she said. "We've been together since we were sixteen years old."

Looking over at her, I didn't know whether to be angry with her or to feel sorry for her—or to feel nothing at all. I was convinced that Shannon had no idea how deeply involved I was with the new woman in my life. A woman she knew well.

Once at the event, I went into masquerade mode, acting as though everything in our marriage was perfect. Donning an emotional "mask" was no stretch for me. I had been playing various roles all my life, trying to gain acceptance. We greeted people, hugged, smiled, and danced together. We both sensed it wasn't the right time or place to make a scene, so I continued living the lie.

No one would have suspected I was having a sexual affair with one of my wife's best friends. Sometimes I didn't believe it myself, and if anyone would have asked me at that time to explain my actions and feelings, I would have been unable to do so. Who can adequately explain the anatomy of an affair? Oh, sure, I could spout the usual platitudes and excuses, but they fell far short of explaining what was really going on in my heart and mind. Looking back, I now know that my sexual "indiscretions" began years before I entered a bedroom with a woman who was not my wife.

Some say, "Hope is where the heart is." Well, I didn't see any hope for this marriage.

CHAPTER 2

WE ARE ALL MESSED UP

'm convinced that everybody is messed up. Some of us are screwed up by our own choices; many of us are negatively affected by actions or attitudes our parents or grandparents foisted on us. I know for sure that Shannon and I were a mess. Without wishing to attribute blame or avoid personal responsibility, I believe much of our dysfunction began with the decisions and actions of our parents and grandparents, choices over which we had no control. Although they didn't do it intentionally, our families unwittingly set us up for failure.

I never knew how a real family functioned. I had little sense of belonging within my nuclear family. Early in life, I felt I was a trophy kid who my parents pulled out when they wanted to impress their friends. I was musically talented, and at two years of age, I sang songs with my mom in church. I carried a tune pretty well. The songs were simple, spiritual ditties and other well-known children's songs, such as "Jesus Loves Me" and "This Little Light of Mine," and I sang them with gusto! My parents were so proud of me for being able to perform at such a young age, and they lavished me with praise.

Dad was a hard worker with great personal charisma, but he was quiet and reserved at home. Maybe that stemmed from the fact that he never felt connected to his own family while growing up. His mom, "Maw" Pourteau, my paternal grandmother, was not a warm and fuzzy person. She was old school, lived in the country, and adopted three boys who became her life. My dad wasn't one of them. Dad felt slighted and that the adopted sons were more worthy of love than he was. Rather than feeling he was an integral part of his family sharing love with three boys who desperately needed it, he found himself on the outside.

They lived in the small town of Reeves, Louisiana, between Lake Charles and Shreveport, where Dad's family owned and operated a couple of logging trucks. Several of our extended family members were loggers, and a couple of them suffered tragic accidents while on the job. While at work one day, my paternal grandfather backed over his youngest son with a logging truck, killing him instantly. The week before his wedding, my uncle slipped and fell on a chainsaw, nearly shearing his leg from his body. He lived for a week after the accident before dying. My grandfather himself was killed when a large branch snapped from a tree, striking him in the head.

Dad quit school as a teenager and worked on a farm. He joined the U.S. Air Force shortly after he turned eighteen and became the top air-traffic controller in his division while stationed in Labrador, Alaska. After receiving his honorable discharge from the military, he parlayed the skills he had learned into starting a successful construction company. He earned a good living and built a comfortable home for my family. Dad was an exceptional provider and is still the go-to guy for his family.

"Uncle Duddy," as Dad is known to our extended family, was not only a go-getter but also a great *giver*. He was incredibly generous, especially considering that he was not a wealthy man himself. He freely passed out wads of money to family members who needed it. Although some of our relatives were ripping off our dad, that didn't seem to bother him. He was always overjoyed to give. Perhaps it was his way of saying, "I love you." It was certainly his way of helping to resolve conflicts.

Even in later years when I confronted him about our relatives using him to get money, Dad said, "Son, they can't use me. I'm giving the money to them."

Besides passing out cash, Dad had a great gift of humor and a self-effacing way of making people laugh. Consequently, he was sort of a showpiece for his family. Everybody loved him.

Dad's side of the family attended United Pentecostal churches, which consisted of ultraconservative, strict, legalistic rule-keepers who believed in the supernatural manifestations of the Spirit—and, occasionally, in the exuberant displays of their own spirits when the genuine Spirit seemed absent. The congregation was accustomed to whooping and hollering, sharing and receiving prophecies (the speaking out of "words" purportedly from God), and even speaking in tongues (unlearned languages), similar to what happened in the Bible. Don't get me wrong: these people were not fakes or charlatans. Many of their spiritual experiences were authentic. Some were misguided or leaned toward a more emotional jag rather than the real thing. But almost all of the people were sincere and believed in the power of prayer and were open to the supernatural. Even my dad was.

My mom came from a "Four Square" religious background, a small Christian denomination similar to the Assemblies of God and to old-time Methodists. Her family lived across from the church and was in attendance anytime it was open. Pawpaw, my maternal grandfather, was the youth minister in the church and was loved by all. He wrote plays that were performed by the youth of the church, and although he wasn't an accomplished singer, he regularly led the "song service," enthusiastically waving his hand above his head in time with the music or pounding his palm on the pulpit to the beat of an old hymn.

My grandma Gagee (pronounced Gay-Gee), who spoke only Cajun French until the third grade when she learned English, taught Sunday school classes, and often sang "specials" requested by members of the congregation. Both of my maternal grandparents were strong believers in God and lived accordingly. They were conservative, and their teachings overflowed with strict, biblical morality. Pawpaw and Grandma Gagee were solid people, but, similar to my dad, Mom felt less worthy of love because she thought her mom loved her brother more than her. There was the disconnect. So the pattern was set for her life—and mine.

As I said, everyone is screwed up. We are products of our home life, and most of us drag around a bunch of baggage: some that we inherited, some that was forced on us.

In her younger years, Mom was a beauty queen with no academic training. She and Dad got together right out of high school and in a short time got married. Dad took a job at Olin Chemical Company to support them. Neither Mom nor Dad had any understanding of what a strong marriage is. I came along, and then Marcus three and a half years later. So like most families, we plodded along as best we could.

Our family attended our grandparents' church in Big Lake, Louisiana, a small congregation of about sixty people. The Pourteau family went to church regularly, almost obsessively. Views on fidelity and marriage were ironclad; marriage was sacred and forever, no matter how miserable a couple might be. The only way out of an ill-advised or nonfunctioning marriage was adultery. Then— and only then—could the "innocent" party, the man or woman who had not been unfaithful to the marriage, get divorced without feeling as though he or she had disobeyed God.

Dad taught Sunday school classes and sometimes sang solos in our church services, as did Mom. Although much of what we were taught to believe had to do with the afterlife—heaven or hell—we were also told that we could trust God for anything, especially for physical healing. When someone in our church got sick, the norm was not to call for a doctor but to call for the pastor. At one point, Dad got extremely ill as the result of a chemical plant meltdown, and he almost died. Part of the reason Dad got so sick was because he had gone back into the plant to rescue others and to shut down the system before it resulted in further destruction. He saved the plant and other lives by sacrificing his own well-being.

Brother Salzman (the pastor of the church in Big Lake) and some elders (spiritual leaders in the church) came to the hospital, anointed Dad with oil, and prayed for him—*loudly* prayed for him, as though God were deaf and two thousand miles away. Dad experienced a miraculous turnaround as God healed him. But Dad didn't want to work at the chemical plant any longer. That's when he started his own construction business. It turned out to be a good move in faith, resulting in a business that prospered.

There were only two times when we attended church—when we felt like it and when we didn't. Every Sunday our family was in church, both morning and evening services. Following the benediction, we usually went to our grandparents' house for lunch. Our relationship with Pawpaw and Gagee was probably the closest model of a genuine family that I saw during my childhood. Pawpaw worshipped my grandma. They loved each other and wanted to be together all the time. We enjoyed fabulous family times with them, especially at Christmas.

After Gagee's delicious meals, the family sat around the table telling stories, laughing, and enjoying each other. We talked over each other in separate conversations that went back and forth. It was a fun, loving atmosphere and a hilarious and enjoyable time for all of us. Because of his quiet nature, however, Dad could handle only small portions of the festivities and usually retired to another room to watch football games on television rather than trying to speak louder than others packed into the room.

Pawpaw had built the house many years earlier for around five thousand dollars, a price thought to be rather exorbitant at the time. The house had three small bedrooms and one bathroom, but my grandparents kept it neat and well maintained. To me, it was a mansion and a place of adventure.

Pawpaw made toys for Marcus and me out of whatever resources he had available. He built a small airplane to scale out of scrap wood he had laying around. The plane couldn't fly, but it was a toy I always played with at our grandparents' home.

Before bedtime, after tucking us in, Pawpaw often told my brother and me tall tales about two little boys who were playing in an abandoned house or junkyard. He could spin grand, magical adventure stories off the cuff, and he enthralled Marcus and me with them until we drifted off to sleep thinking about those two little boys.

Papaw had been forced into early retirement due to an injury. Although he and Gagee lived frugally and had few luxuries, Pawpaw always found something extra to place in our hands every time we saw him. He was the kind of man who brought joy to everyone he met. I often thought, *If I can be like anyone in the world, it would be my Pawpaw.* To me, he was the epitome of a good, Christian man.

We weren't rich, but our family was considered upper-middle class because Dad had helped our aunt open a successful burger place and Mom ran a little dress boutique. Most of the people living nearby probably thought we were wealthy. When you grow up in "the country," it is hard to tell who has money and who doesn't. Folks don't flash cash around. But people knew that we were doing okay. After all, Dad was a Ford truck guy, and those pickups weren't cheap, and everyone knew that Dad was good at what he did. He was not only a contractor; he was a builder. He built from scratch our comfortable, two-story home, which also had a big yard.

I never saw or heard my parents argue. Nor did I ever hear my father raise his voice toward my mother. It seemed to me that Mom and Dad had a great marriage. Unfortunately, I was wrong.

One day, when I was eight years old, Mom called to my brother, Marcus, and me. "Boys, come upstairs. I want to talk with you." She led us into the bedroom and had me sit on the bed and Marcus in her lap as she told us, "Mom and Dad are going to separate, and Dad is going away." I wasn't even sure what that meant, but my brother and I guessed that something awful had happened. Or maybe he or I had done something horrible. Why else would Dad be leaving?

Dad and Mom eventually divorced. I didn't understand. During my early childhood, I didn't even know anyone who had been divorced or how divorce might affect our family's living circumstances. All I knew was that Mom cried a lot, so I tried to comfort her as best I could.

"You have to be the man in the family now, Jimmy," she told me through her tears with her arms wrapped tightly around me.

I was eight; what did I know about being the man in the family? Maybe Mom thought that extra burden would help me to buck up and be strong and not allow myself to cry or be sad because Dad was gone. She didn't say, and I didn't ask. But I felt the load on my shoulders.

When Mom and Dad split up, we plummeted from an upper-middle-class status to poor overnight. To help support us, Mom always managed to find some man who might take care of her and, by extension, my brother and me.

Maybe my parents' divorce opened the emotional floodgates for my mother. During my early years, she married eleven or more times—so many times that I can't even remember the names of all her husbands. She had two things going for her: her striking physical beauty and her unusual moral code, by which she deemed it acceptable to divorce and remarry nearly a dozen times. But she wouldn't sleep around or have an affair outside of marriage.

Before you pass judgment on her, please remember this: we're all screwed up. There are vulnerabilities that influence us toward certain ways of thinking. One thing I know for sure is that the way a person thinks is how he or she will do life.

Dad didn't talk about the divorce. He never discussed anything with Marcus or me about his leaving. He simply disappeared, or at least it seemed that way to me. I hardly ever saw him, spent little time with him, talked with him only on occasion, and rarely knew where he was or what he was doing—until my early teens when we connected again after he remarried. His new wife, Karen, encouraged him to renew contact with us.

I had no relationship with any of our relatives on my dad's side of the family, partly because I felt abandoned by my father and my relatives, and partly because I hated the way our relatives used him to get money. My only male family member that I recall liking was Uncle "Buddy," Mom's brother who was a mere ten years older than I was but seemed like an adult to me. More importantly, he seemed to respect me and treated me well.

Uncle Buddy made me laugh. He was a jokester with a quick, sharp wit, someone who picked on me and teased me. But I always knew that he would give or do anything for the people he loved, and that included me.

One night, Uncle Buddy and my Aunt Melinda went out dancing at a saloon-type dance hall in Lake Charles, and I tagged along. Back in those days, it was not unusual for adults to have kids accompany them to a bar or dance hall. Although I was a big kid and looked older than my age, I was barely thirteen. But the bartender had few qualms about fulfilling my requests for another beer and later a Bloody Mary.

While Uncle Buddy and Aunt Melinda were out on the dance floor, I ran into "Jim," one of Mom's old consorts. He looked surprised to see me, and I suspected that he recognized me. "Jimmy?" he asked. I knew I was busted.

"Hey," I replied bashfully.

Mom's former boyfriend smiled when he saw me holding a drink, and his eyes sparkled playfully. "Whatcha drinking, Big Man?" he asked sarcastically.

I didn't know squat about alcoholic beverages or their labels, but I cocked my head and blurted the first thing that came to mind. "Crème de Menthe," I replied.

Bad choice.

"Well, great. Let's get you another." Mom's friend guided me back to the bar. "Give my man here another Crème de Menthe," he said with a twinkle in his eyes.

The bartender looked at me, looked at my glass, then back at Mom's friend with a smile. He loaded up a glass with the thick, green mint ingredients, and Mom's friend watched as I downed it. No doubt, there was an explosion in my stomach when the mint mixed with the Bloody Mary that I had been drinking and sloshed around with the beer that was already there.

All I know is that whatever was inside me came out that night! I spent most of the night under the kitchen table, puking my guts out.

Rather than learning from the experience, I looked forward to hanging out and experiencing more of "life" with older people. Not surprisingly, I was out with a group of adults when I ingested my first dose of acid. We were canoeing on the Whiskey-Chitter River, and I was getting tired. To keep me going, I took a microdot of acid that dissolved on my tongue. Not only did it keep me going, I rowed like I had a power motor on my back! Unfortunately, I was so agitated and rowing so erratically, I flipped the canoe over and dumped all of our food into the water. The sandwiches floated on down the river.

So what do you do when you are too "speedy" to slow down and you've lost all your food? You smoke a joint. Before long, we forgot all about our missing food supply.

Certainly, dysfunctional people in my life aided and abetted my ascendency into adulthood without the maturity meant to accompany it. But the one who influenced me most was my mom.

Mom grew increasingly manic in her behavior and could instantly become quite volatile. She'd go from a beaming countenance with all smiles to whipping Marcus or me, wielding a piece of Hot Wheels racetrack as a belt. Those little guardrails and the underside of the racetrack left some serious welts on my butt and back. Actually, Mom grabbed anything close and used it to swat at us. She wasn't afraid of her boys as we grew older either. At sixteen years of age, I mouthed off to Mom, and when I turned away from her, she literally leaped onto my back and said, "Boy, I don't care how big you get. You will always respect me, even if I have to draw it out of you with a two by four!"

I believed her.

At times, Mom was my greatest cheerleader. "You can do anything, Jimmy!" she'd gush. But then, almost in the same breath, she'd stand outside and yell at me, "What's wrong with you? Get your fat ass out here!" That term of endearment was her favorite nickname for me, and she referred to me by it often. For years, I thought my middle name was "Fat Ass."

"You're so lazy!" Mom would rail at me.

But an hour later, she'd be pumping me full of her tripe again. "Oh, Jimmy, you can do anything you put your mind to doing."

Mom's back-and-forth behavior created some indelible finger-prints on my life. I'm sorry to say that over the years, I have some-times repeated that sort of behavior with people I love.

• • • • •

My mom's grandmother, MereMere', was a tubby old French-Cajun pioneer, rough around the edges. She ran a bar when she was younger. My great-grandfather was an alcoholic and was abu-sive to MereMere'. They lived by Big Lake, a short drive from our house when I was a little boy. She eventually dumped PerePere', her abusive husband, and moved to Lake Charles. But she still had a tough life.

Regardless, that was no excuse for what she did to me.

I sometimes stayed in her home with her during the day, and she often looked at me in the middle of the afternoon and said, "You need a bath. Let's go get a bath."

She then stripped off her clothes and mine and put me into the bathtub with her. Today most child psychologists don't consider it anything weird for toddlers to take a bath with parents or even to sleep in the same bed with Mom and Dad during those early years. But this was different. Great-Grandmother ordered me to get out of my clothes and to sit down in the bathtub with her, and then she encouraged me to touch her vagina. I had no notion that anything I was doing was wrong or that she was sick for wanting me to do such a thing. She was simply my great-grandmother and was an authority figure in my childhood, so if she told me to do something, I usually obeyed.

She began these "special baths" when I was four or five years old, and after the baths, I distinctly recall lying next to her on her bed, her breasts exposed for me to touch. Nobody knew what she was doing with me, and for years I never told anyone, not even my mom.

It would be years later when I began wondering what sort of impact those experiences had in my life. My Uncle Buddy and I talked about it in vague terms. "There was definitely some weirdness there," Buddy recalled.

No kidding.

In an odd way, I was glad to learn that my memories of Great-Grandmother were not the fabrications of my overactive imagination.

I can't help but wonder if one of the effects of her sexually molesting me led to early promiscuity in my life. When I was ten years old, a female cousin who was eight years older than me let me explore her body and took great pleasure in mine.

My first experience of actual sexual intercourse was completely nondescript and unexciting. An older girl named Kathy and I "did the deed," although I wasn't quite sure what that meant. She sometimes played with me in the church nursery—and she wasn't playing jacks or pickup sticks. Later, I realized I had lost my virginity with her, but to this day I have no recollection of where or when it happened. But it did.

About the time I turned twelve, a fellow named Marvin, who attended another church nearby, sometimes took me out hunting with him. He was old enough to drive, so I felt privileged that he wanted me to hang out with him. But that wasn't all he wanted. Marvin was sexually abusive to me as well.

While it might seem strange that I would allow these people to take advantage of me sexually, it's important to understand that their actions did not seem wrong to me. I was thrilled that they gave me attention. Their warped desires provided warm bodies that made me feel good and, more importantly, wanted. I didn't feel dirty about what was happening; quite the contrary, I felt *significant*, that somebody liked me and wanted me to be with them. I felt as though I mattered.

I hardly ever heard any teaching from the church about sex, other than learning that premarital or extramarital sex was sin and I needed to repent for even thinking about it, much less for engaging in any sort of sexual activity as a kid. I didn't get it. I couldn't connect the "wrongness" with the good feelings I experienced from feeling wanted. As the songs on the radio reminded me, "How could it be wrong when it feels so right?"

The Pentecostal message back then was replete with rules and prohibitions; most messages tilted toward the negative rather than the good things God has done or is willing to do in our lives. Pentecostals worried more about burning in hell than living positively now on earth. The church provided me with a strong incentive: "Do right or you will be ostracized." That sort of avoidance motive usually produces a controlling nature—I know it did in me.

We learned little about grace (the unmerited favor of God), and while we were encouraged to seek the forgiveness of God, less was said about forgiving those who hurt us. Hardly anything was taught about forgiving ourselves. Instead, our hyper-charismatic teachers and preachers regaled us with such biblical "wisdom" as "Don't trust doctors . . . if you do, you don't have faith."

Yet it was okay in our circles to need a physical healing, whether it was for the flu or a broken arm. It was also okay to go to the doctor for diabetes, cancer, or other physical maladies. But if your problem was mental or emotional, struggling with anxiety, depression, or unexplained fears, that was "spiritual" and quite possibly even the result of demonic oppression, and you needed deliverance from that. Don't dare even think that God cares about your emotional health or that you might need more or less serotonin or some medication in your system to avoid depression (as I discovered years later that I did). Some of the pastors I heard spouted such outrageous statements as, "If you are sleeping with Prince Valium, you don't know the Jesus I know! If you go home today and turn on your TV, and you don't come back to church tonight, I pray that your television blows up right in your face!"

It didn't occur to me that I needed to be fixed for any of these emotional or spiritual issues, but I knew something was different about our family.

CHAPTER 3

DIVORCE FALLOUT

Not long after our parents divorced, Mom met her first "next" husband, Amir, a Lebanese immigrant who ran a restaurant and lounge in the area. I heard he had some connection to the Mafia and that his own brother was killed in a gangland-styled hit.

Unfortunately, shortly after Mom and Amir married, their relationship soured. Mom and our new stepdad turned brutal toward each other—fighting, hitting, and even jumping on each other. I was just a kid, but whenever I saw Amir going after my mom, I jumped in between them. "Don't hit my mom!" I screamed at him.

Mom marrying an Arab fellow was rather odd, especially since some of our family members were Southern rednecks, who were as prejudiced against Arabs as they were against Blacks.

We lived in an apartment right next to the sewage plant. The walls were paper thin, so when Mom and Amir argued—which they did often—my friends outside could hear the fighting. I tried to downplay the seriousness of the noise to my friends or anyone within hearing distance. "He just won a lot of money betting on a game," I explained, "and they are probably celebrating." It was a blatant lie.

I developed a penchant for lying, usually to present myself as a different sort of person, hiding behind walls that I had erected to protect the real me. On one side of the wall, there was a picture of the person I hoped other people might love and accept if I acted the way they expected; behind the wall on my side was the real me.

At the same time, I was motivated to achieve success and significance, not so much from a desire for excellence but out of an avoidance of failure. I wanted to do things so I could not be ignored. If I was in a school choir, I wanted to win the state championship.

I was the best actor in our high school competitions because I was accustomed to pretending. "How'd you get into character?" somebody might ask me.

"I don't know," I'd say. "I was just playing a part." So I grew adept at playing parts and creating roles for myself, whether they were based in truth and reality or not. If something made me feel significant and that I mattered, I would do it. That sort of significance was self-defeating, however. I could never do or obtain enough to feel that I possessed intrinsic worth.

My schoolteachers were unaware of my inner conflict because I looked as though I had it all together. At school, I wore nice, country club golf clothes because Dad was a good golfer who probably could have played on the pro circuit. He never did, but he played in a lot of golf tournaments and won lots of clothes, which he passed on to Marcus and me on the few occasions when we would see him. Perhaps that was Dad's way of demonstrating his love and support for my brother and me.

Marcus and I were on our own a lot. So I took care of Marcus, watching out for him and making sure that other kids didn't take advantage of him. My friends were always a diverse bunch when we lived near the sewer plant. In fact, for two years of our lives,

Marcus and I, along with Monique, a white girl, were the only white kids living in a predominantly Black neighborhood. I was a good talker, so I got along wherever I went.

Unfortunately, Mom tended to get gutter guys. She saw herself as deserving only that sort of person. Even though she was physically beautiful, she always felt that the guys wouldn't stay, and they didn't.

So I would try to be the man of the house . . . until she'd meet another man. Then I felt pushed out of my position. The message I received was that I must not be doing a very good job. So I spent the rest of my life trying to earn acceptance and do whatever was necessary to cause someone to need and want me.

When the next man would go away, I'd have to step up again. Mom repeatedly used that influence to get me to do whatever she wanted me to do.

I didn't rebel against the men in my mom's life. Truth is, I didn't really care enough about them to rebel, because I assumed they didn't care about me. In most cases, I was right.

Mom never tried to explain her relationships to Marcus and me—whether her new beau was a Mafia member, rancher, race car driver, drug addict, or whoever. I didn't go to any of Mom's marriage ceremonies. Years later, she asked me to serve as the minister to marry her to some loser. He was a "preacher" named Gus, and he and Mom connected at church somehow. He "prophesied over" Mom, and she became enamored with his spirituality. I didn't like him, and I told him so because he was so fake. He was always Mr. Spiritual, quoting the Bible and telling Marcus and me what it meant in Hebrew or Greek.

Gus represented everything that many people loathe about Christians. He had "words of prophecy" for everyone else, encouraging them to clean up their lives, but apparently, traits such as self-control and discipline did not apply to him. He was grossly overweight and was supposedly on a diet, but he would surreptitiously sneak around the kitchen, searching for cake or chips or anything he could stuff into his mouth. He scarfed up food like a powerful vacuum cleaner and usually smeared food all around his mouth. He was the picture of indiscipline. He said good things but never did them. Mom may have seen something attractive about him, but I had no respect for him.

While I was still in sixth grade, Mom moved to Houston and took a job as a secretary. She lived and worked there on her own for a full year. Meanwhile, Marcus and I remained behind until Mom could get established. We lived with our grandparents in the country. When Mom finally felt ready for us, Marcus and I followed her to Texas.

Houston was huge and far away from our small town where everyone knew us, so Mom felt it would be a good place to start over. She worked hard and was never lazy. Even though we were broke, Mom seemed upbeat about her fresh start. We lived in a small apartment for a while, and it was there that we celebrated our first Christmas in Texas, one of only three Christmases we celebrated anywhere when I was a child. Prior to that first Christmas, I remember only one Christmas present my family ever gave me—my uncle gave me a Star Trek phaser gun when I was in fifth grade. On our first Christmas in Texas, Mom bought me a pair of sneaker-skates and a cowboy hat with a feather on the side, along with some cowboy boots. She did something similar for Marcus. That's all we could afford. Many of our scant evening meals at that time involved pork and beans on bread. I actually grew to like the combination. I didn't realize that the reason Mom served it so often was because we were so poor.

I was working by the time I was twelve years old, landing my first job as a host at Los Tios Mexican restaurant in Houston. Many of our customers were not native Texans. Instead, they hailed from across the border. Some were living in the country legally, others were not. I couldn't speak a word of Spanish, but as I mentioned, I was friendly. I looked older than my competitors, so I lied about my age and got the job. I worked hard and had fun at the same time. I enjoyed the Hispanic people, and they seemed to like me. Maybe our poverty bound us together in a common understanding.

In Houston, I attended Memorial Junior High through seventh and then eighth grade—twice. I was an average student during my first eight years of school. Then, at thirteen years of age, I failed eighth grade, mainly because I was stoned and sluggish for most of that year due to the marijuana I bought from friends and began smoking regularly.

Mom must have known about me getting high, but we never had a conversation about it. She had enough problems in her own life. So, not surprisingly, when I started drinking alcohol around that same time, she didn't mention that either.

I also discovered pornography with mom's new husband, Richard, who sold law books, lived in a great condominium, and drove a Chrysler New Yorker. I was thirteen and in eighth grade. VCRs were popular, and Richard had one when we moved in with him. He'd buy videotaped cartoons for Marcus and me to watch. On one occasion, I put in a tape and it wasn't a cartoon; it was a pornographic movie, *Debby Does Dallas*. I had never before seen such a thing! There was no Internet back then, so my friends who were more "adventurous" often made a big deal about procuring a *Playboy* magazine from their big brothers or their moms' boyfriends. Imagine how my status with them soared when I brought my friends over to our house and popped in a pornographic video! Entrepreneur that I was, I charged them to watch it.

Other than watching his dirty movies, I never got close to Richard. The one time I did, he kicked me down the stairs. I had been coughing, and Richard confronted me about it, claiming that

I was coughing too much. We got into an argument and I lost, finding myself at the bottom of the stairs. But I put up with him as the new man.

I had few positive role models during those years. But one person who made a difference in my life was a curly-haired social studies teacher who looked like actor Gabe Kaplan, star of the 1970s sitcom *Welcome Back, Kotter*. At the start of my second year in his class, he greeted me, "Welcome back, Pourteau." He paid attention to me and helped me get through the year. He didn't let me get away with anything, but neither did he look at me as a bad kid. He encouraged me to use the intelligence God had given to me. Had it not been for him, I may have quit school after eighth grade. When I finally made it out of junior high, I moved on to Stratford High School.

In high school, Rob Seible, a school choir teacher with whom I still stay in contact, also took an interest in me. He didn't try to force me into some sort of arbitrary mold that wasn't me. He never talked down to me but always spoke kindly to me and with respect. "Just sing, Jim," he said. So I did.

He loved music and led the choir at his church for years without missing a single Sunday. Interestingly, Mr. Seible was gay. He did not flaunt his sexual preferences or attempt to force his lifestyle on anyone else; nor did he try to influence his students to follow his example. According to my church, Mr. Seible was the sort of fellow I should avoid and regard with disdain, yet he was one of the few men in my early life who exhibited unabashed acceptance and kindness toward me. Although I didn't understand his sexual choices, I benefited greatly from his instruction and guidance.

With Mr. Seible's encouragement, I not only learned to sing well but also learned to play several instruments. I didn't take formal music lessons; we really couldn't afford that sort of luxury, so I bought a Roy Clark guitar songbook and taught myself how to play guitar. I also learned to play bass guitar, keyboards, and drums, so before long, I got involved in the music program at church. I guessed my participation pleased my mom. I actually wanted to take part. I liked it, and performing in church gave me a sense of fulfillment.

I was gregarious and talkative, so I was fairly popular with my classmates. Many of my peers were already interested in sex, as was I. So I assumed most young women my age wanted to engage in some form of sexual activity. I didn't realize that sex was not necessarily a given, an expected, almost mandatory part of the pre-marital relationship.

I didn't date, at least not in the ordinary sense. I went out with girls and had sex but did not have meaningful relationships. I didn't feel that I was using the young women, but no doubt, we were using each other. For instance, a girl named Jamie applied my makeup for one of the school plays, so we had sex in her cramped compact car, to the tune of "Her Little Red Corvette." I was the quintessential "Slam, Bam, thank you, ma'am" sort of guy, and I didn't even know it.

Again, Mom may have realized that I was having sex, but she never mentioned it. She focused on providing for us, and when she wasn't working at her job, she was working overtime to attract a new man. Mom was gone a lot and kept up with me even less after I started driving. My dad gave me an old 1978 Chrysler Cordoba with velour seats. The muffler was falling off, the air-conditioning in the car did not work—in Houston of all places—nor did the radio, so I installed a new sound system in it, rolled the windows down, and let the music blare. The gas-guzzler wasn't much to look at, but it represented freedom to me, and I was grateful for it.

I was a worker. I worked anyplace I could find a job— McDonald's, Pango's Pizza Shop, Popeyes; I even sold vacuum cleaners for a while. I was never lazy or a slacker. I used most of the money I earned for gasoline and car insurance. When the

Cordoba bit the dust, Dad came to the rescue again and bought me another car, a 1979 Toyota Corolla. It wasn't new, but it did have air-conditioning!

By now we lived in a safer area, and Stratford was a good school academically and a 5-A school in sports. Most of my friends were from more affluent families in much higher financial brackets than ours, so I felt insecure and inadequate. I played fullback and linebacker on our school football team. I didn't play football because I felt compelled to be in sports or had a passionate desire to be an athlete. I played football to be noticed.

I was a decent player but not great. I started out playing in the offensive guard position. On our team, that meant I was a "pulling guard," pulling out of my position, charging behind the center and leading the blockers into the defensive line, and hopefully blasting a hole through which our running backs could carry the football. Mine was an important role but with no real recognition, other than getting the daylights beat out of me by the defense. High school football in Texas is tough, and although I was a strong 190 pounds, I got banged up all the time.

When an opportunity came up for me to move to the defensive linebacker position, I took it. After all, our middle linebacker called the defensive plays. I worked diligently to rise to the leadership position because the leader gets to tell others what to do. You can't ignore me. I enjoyed playing fullback even more. My job was usually to plow through the line and hit the first linebacker I could see.

My main reason for playing sports had little to do with taking out my aggression or impressing my female classmates. I wanted to attract my dad's attention. Dad hadn't played organized sports when he was a kid, but he was a sports nut.

Every season, I hoped my dad might come to see me play. He never did.

THE MARRIAGE
OF MY DREAMS

CHAPTER 4

SPIRITUAL AWAKENING

For most people, spiritual awakening is a cumulative process. As a teenager, I went to church camp and began understanding more about why the gospel made sense. I became a real Christian at sixteen, and as all Christians do, my transformation began with a Jewish fellow—but not the one you may think.

In high school, I often hung out with a guy named Scott, who I met in my drama and acting classes. Scott had only one eye—he never spoke about what had happened to the other—and he had been adopted into a Jewish family. I loved going to his house because the food was fantastic, especially at holiday time, and they had more food holidays than anyone I knew.

Scott wanted to be a professional dancer, and I teased him incessantly that he needed to pursue something more realistic. "Dude, you only have one eye. You're going to dance right into a pole!"

Scott and I were still sixteen years old when he introduced me to his friend Nathan, a guy in his early twenties who looked as though he were a California surfer dude with his wavy blond hair and movie star good looks. We often went to the mall together, and

Nathan would take his guitar and sing to the girls to help us pick up dates. We'd later get stoned together. Since I had been working from the time I was twelve or thirteen, I usually had cash, and Nathan knew just where we could spend it.

One Friday, Nathan shocked us. He said, "I've been to a tent revival and I found Christ."

"You found what?" Scott asked. He had no idea what Nathan was talking about. But I did. With my Pentecostal background, I understood perfectly well where Nathan had been and what he had done.

But if the initial news surprised me, his next statement sent me reeling. "Yeah, I found Jesus," he said, "so I don't want to party anymore."

Nathan, are you serious? I thought.

I grew up as a regular church attender. But church attendance hadn't done much for my family or for me. My family was a mess, in spite of practically living at the sanctuary. I'd been to church camp, too, and revival meetings, and I thought I'd seen and heard it all. But this was different. This was not religious hype; this was real, and Nathan's comments hit me like a brick.

After all, Nathan didn't need Jesus. He wasn't a down-and-outer, or an up-and-outer; he wasn't a loser in any sense of the word. He was smart, good-looking, and popular. Why would he need Jesus?

"I'll hang out with you guys," Nathan said, "but I'm not going to smoke dope with you anymore. There are some things I want to change."

Although I was impressed, I was also perplexed. Nathan's words bothered me. In a good way, they gnawed at the callousness covering my heart, poking holes in my veneer, clearing an opening, a pathway to my soul. I had never really thought of God as a loving Being. I didn't connect with the idea of God as a heavenly Father.

To me, He was more like the giant foot in Monty Python movies, poised above my head ready to stomp on me whenever I made a mistake. But Nathan had found something much different in his faith than I had ever discovered.

Later that night, sitting alone in my bedroom, I had a conversation with God—well, it was actually more like a monologue than a conversation. Still, I laid out my feelings honestly to God, as well as to myself.

I couldn't get away from the thought, *Nathan doesn't need religion. Why did he decide to follow Jesus?*

By this time, Mom was married to a race car driver, Vonn Moody, and she seemed happy, but she suffered from persistent, debilitating migraine headaches almost every night. So as I talked to God, I could hear Mom in the next room whimpering in pain from her migraine. I reminded God, "Mom said that when I was a kid, I prayed for her when things really mattered. I'm not sure anymore that You are even real. Can You just show me that You are real? That all of this—what happened to Nathan—and all the rest, really matters?" I didn't know any fancy way to pray, so I just shot straight with God. He didn't seem to mind.

I went to Mom's room and prayed for her. Specifically, I spoke in simple terms, "God, would You take Mom's headache away?" To my amazement, before I left her room, Mom was happy and smiling. "Jimmy, my headache is gone!" she said.

Not only did it go away, but she never had another migraine. I knew her miraculous relief was not because of me, so I deduced logically, "God, You must be real."

That night, in my room, all by myself, I gave my life to Christ. I knew the drill, how to pray, and I had some biblical knowledge, but this was not some rote repetition, nor was it an emotional jag for me; this was real. I knelt down next to my bed and said, "God, I will give You my life." I meant it.

I started attending Church of the Southwest, an Assemblies of God congregation in Houston, and began serving in the church. By now, I was almost seventeen years old and had discovered a genuine relationship with God.

I lost track of Nathan since he didn't go to church with us. But I found several other Christian "brothers" who I hung out with.

My youth pastor, Steve Warriner, had a profound influence on me. He and his wife, Melanie, were both about five foot tall and had a couple of kids and looked like kids themselves. But they loved each other and they loved me. Steve was about twelve years older than I was, and he took me everywhere with him. He didn't preach at me or try to mentor me overtly. He didn't have any preconceived notions of what I should be, but I felt certain that he really cared about me as a person.

"Jimmy, I believe in you," Steve often said. "Let's try this." Then he might make a suggestion about some aspect of my life.

I hadn't heard those words, "I believe in you," from anyone else. They created an instant affinity, and I deeply wanted to please Steve and Melanie. We didn't do anything fancy. We just hung out together and ate Mexican food. But by his example, Steve showed me how to live a Christian life.

Mike Walker, a single guy who worked in Houston as a nuclear medical technician, also helped with the youth group kids, and I'd hang out with him as well. Mike was in his early thirties, drove a Lincoln Mark 5 luxury automobile, and was a decent guitar player. We hit it off, and he took an interest in guiding me.

Except for two teachers in school, Steve and Mike were the first adult males who treated me well without wanting something from me.

When our church youth group decided to take a ski trip to Keystone, Colorado, I knew Mom couldn't afford to pay for it, and

I didn't have much in my savings, either. But the youth were selling gummy bears to raise money for the trip, so I became the best gummy bear salesman in Houston!

I never thought of myself as poor. I didn't feel oppressed or downtrodden. I didn't feel bad about my circumstances. My attitude was, "That's just the way it is." I viewed all of my experiences, whether positive or negative, as "It's just life."

CHAPTER 5

ROCK SOLID

I was sixteen, and since I could sing and played guitar fairly well, Steve Warriner invited me to join the church worship band. Then he took it a step further. "Let's form a youth worship band," Steve suggested, "so we can play for our youth group activities and include some more contemporary music." That sounded good to me. Steve was great at helping me feel accepted. I was slightly older than some of the other kids in our youth group, so although I was relatively new in the faith, I was an instant leader.

We wrote and performed some of our own rock 'n' roll songs with Christian lyrics, made T-shirts with our band logo on them, and even traveled to other churches to play for their youth.

Steve was a great encourager. He was as close to being an advocate for me as anyone I ever knew in my life. He rarely told me to do something; his usual tack was, "Try this." I felt close to Steve and trusted him more than anyone else in my life at that time. I had come to Christ, so I wasn't as rowdy as I had been earlier. Consequently, Steve's influence truly had a tremendous positive impact on me.

I had always wanted to be a doctor, so during my sophomore year in high school, I joined a medical career study group called Health Occupation Science Association (HOSA). Medicine piqued my interest and came naturally to me, so the HOSA leaders helped me get a job I could work after school and on weekends at Rosewood General Hospital. I assisted as a respiratory therapist. I had already become a CPR instructor and had taught for the American Heart Association.

Although I loved medicine, my heart's desire began changing during my senior year of school. I felt that I wanted to work in some sort of ministry. I talked to Steve about my future career and the schooling I might need, and he and I laid out my options. At the time, Houston Baptist University made an offer to me: "We'll help you get into college in the premed program if you want to stay here."

I was torn. "Medicine or ministry?" I prayed, "God, I need to know what to do."

One Sunday night at church, about fifteen or twenty members of our youth group were praying in a back room after the evening service. Many were asking God to do something fresh in their lives. I walked around the room, stopping to pray for various teenagers in the group, praying brief but specific prayers. I prayed with a kid about his father here, a girl about her boyfriend there, and someone almost always was concerned about the salvation of a loved one, a sister or brother, an aunt or uncle.

Several kids approached me afterward and said, "Jim, how did you know?"

"What do you mean?" I asked. "Know what? What are you talking about?"

"You were praying the exact same things I was asking God about in my life. But how did you know that?"

I didn't. Whatever happened there was beyond me. But I realized that God had used me as a conduit to get His message through to some kids. I wondered, *Maybe there's something for me to do.* Although I am not the one who can fix someone, He can work through me if I allow Him.

Afterward, I talked to Steve about the tug of war going on in my heart and mind, pondering whether to pursue a career in medicine or ministry. Steve listened carefully, then posed an interesting question. "Jim, you've been asking God to show you if He is with you in a certain area. Have you felt that about the medical field?"

"No, I'm interested in it," I admitted, "but I don't feel any sense of calling that I am supposed to be there."

I began thinking more seriously about entering the ministry. I was especially interested in evangelism, presenting the gospel message to people in simple, straightforward terms and inviting them to trust Jesus for themselves. I felt my personality and talents lent themselves to that sort of ministry more than as a pastor.

Certainly, the quintessential evangelist was Billy Graham. He probably preached the gospel to more people than any other human being in history. But while Pentecostals appreciated and respected Billy Graham for his emphasis on evangelism and his own personal integrity, we didn't always regard Billy Graham as highly as he deserved. He was much too inclusive for our legalistic crowd. In his association's follow-up materials—free information given to converts, including a New Testament and some "how to get started as a Christian" sort of literature—the Billy Graham Evangelistic Association (BGEA) did not play favorites. If a person responded to an invitation to meet Christ and checked a box indicating that he or she attended a certain church, BGEA would send helpful information to the person's home church if that congregation was participating in the crusade, even to some churches that were not in the evangelical fold.

Pentecostals were not so altruistic about their new converts.

Evangelist Jimmy Swaggart was a superstar in my denominational church circles. He was on television regularly and traveling the country doing evangelistic crusades. I was fascinated watching and listening to him. He epitomized everything that I thought went along with being a great evangelistic preacher—bold and outspoken to the point of making some people angry. As Abraham Lincoln is purported to have said, "I like a preacher who preaches like he is swatting bees." With perspiration pouring off his face as he waved his Bible and paced the platform, Jimmy Swaggart represented that passion and fire that I saw as essential in a successful evangelist.

I attended a Jimmy Swaggart Crusade in Houston when the charismatic minister came to our city. My pastor was on the crusade setup team, so I volunteered to help. I had already committed my life to Christ, but when I heard Jimmy Swaggart preach and heard him invite people to seal their commitments, I moved toward the front of the arena along with all the new believers. A woman counselor prayed with me. Afterward, she asked, "Do you have a Bible?"

"Not really, no," I replied.

"Here," she said, handing me the worn, obviously well-read Bible she carried. "Let me give you mine."

I thanked her sincerely and used that Bible until it fell apart—and then got the pages and leather jacket rebound. Years later, I gave it to my dad as a Christmas present.

My dad had shown up in my life again by my senior year and offered to pay for me to attend Bible college. I researched some possible schools and was drawn mostly toward Jimmy Swaggart Bible College in Baton Rouge, Louisiana.

Aside from the attraction of Brother Swaggart's own swaggering style of evangelism and his heart to help people who had been hurt, some of the professors there were world changers. One man had built more than sixty churches in Africa—*after* he had turned fifty years of age! Others were serious Bible scholars who could translate and expound on the Scriptures from their original languages.

I knew zero theology. But I wanted to preach and felt that I might have a gift of evangelism, which is a significant part of helping introduce others to Jesus Christ. In my home church, I preached my first sermon, based on 1 Kings 18:21, about the Jewish prophet Elijah challenging the people of God, "How long will you hesitate between two opinions? If the LORD is God, follow Him." Although I wasn't afraid to boldly present the truth, my attitude and messages were always evangelistic, giving hope to people and respite to their lives.

CHAPTER 6

THE WOMAN OF
MY DREAMS

Steve Warriner, Mike, and I were leading a Sunday night service at our church in Houston, and I was on the platform singing and playing guitar during "praise and worship," the portion of the service intended to help people prepare their hearts and minds for the sermon the pastor planned to preach. Between songs, I looked out into the audience and noticed an attractive young woman sitting along the side of the sanctuary. She was dressed casually in jeans and a cute top and seemed somewhat interested— and somewhat guarded—almost as if she didn't know what to expect next.

I leaned over to Mike and nodded toward the attractive young woman. "I think I'm going to ask her out," I said with a smile.

Mike chuckled, rolled his eyes a bit, and we carried on with the music.

I could hardly wait until the service was over so I could get off the platform and meet the girl who had caught my eye. I approached her in a friendly manner and introduced myself.

"Hi, I'm Jim," I said. "I don't think I've seen you here before. Welcome! I'm glad you've come."

The young woman seemed shy and unimpressed with me, but she told me that her name was Shannon. I was instantly attracted to her. This was the kind of woman I wanted. She was a brunette with big, sparkling brown eyes. I later prayed, "Lord, I believe she is the one." I had been praying for a wife with Shannon's sort of hair and eyes. Of course, I noticed her smile and demeanor as well, but those beautiful eyes really got to me. We were taught back then that we had to pray specifically or else God would mess it up—which was not true—but we didn't know any better.

Shannon and I talked briefly and she gave me some basic information about herself. The oldest of three siblings, Shannon didn't attend our church, but her mom and younger siblings, Barry and Sherrie, did. Although I wasn't aware of it at the time, I later discovered that my mom and Shannon's mom were friends, and my brother, Marcus, who was also attending youth group activities at the church, and Shannon's sister, Sherrie, were infatuated with each other.

I also learned that before Shannon and I first met, she had been dating a guy named Alex, who was several years older than she was and employed nearby. She was seriously interested in Alex, apparently, but they had a roller coaster on-again, off-again relationship.

Shannon continued attending the youth group meetings and activities, so we often joined together with groups of other people. Although she didn't seem too interested in me, I was definitely interested in her. On one occasion, Shannon had gone to a girlfriend's house and Alex was there. They were in "off again" mode at the time. She thought that he might want to get back together with her, so it crushed Shannon when the guy made it clear he wasn't interested. Shannon drove home in tears. About that time, I stopped by her house and found her crying her eyes out. I hugged her and attempted to console her. "That guy's missing out," I told her.

We weren't really a couple at that time, but I was hopeful. I wanted to be there for her, to be her friend. Of course, I still hoped to date her.

Not long after that, I asked her out, and within a week or two, Shannon broke off her ties with Alex.

This must be God! I thought.

She was ten months older than me and employed as a dental assistant in a pedodontics office. Her employer highly regarded her and encouraged her to further her education by enrolling in dental hygiene school, which Shannon was considering.

At that time, I was working two part-time jobs. I worked at Rosewood Hospital and also was employed at The Balloon Garden, a boutique balloon and gift shop owned by some people who attended our church. In trying to woo Shannon into my arms, I bought her every size, shape, and color of balloon we carried in the store and repeatedly showered her with bouquets of balloons and other small gifts. The ice began to thaw.

I loved Shannon's easygoing pace. While I was loud and fast, she was slow and quiet. Shannon's personality was that of a pleaser; her priority was to do whatever it took to keep the peace. She is not necessarily a peacemaker, but she is a passionate *peacekeeper*, driven to keep the peace, even if it pains her. She holds her own opinions inside and would rather say, "I don't know" than create an uncomfortable confrontation or make a controversial decision.

Shannon was born in Glasgow, Montana. Her dad, Bill Vukela, served in the US Air Force, so the family moved frequently. Long after her dad's military discharge, when Shannon was in third grade, the family moved again, this time to Sugarland, southwest of Houston, so her dad could work as a salesman for a company that manufactured fire retardant foam used in fighting oil well fires.

As a sixteen-year-old, Shannon worked in a clothing store, and she was arranging clothes on some shelves when she was called to the front of the store because her dad was on the phone. "I'm leaving the family," he told her. "I'm sorry, but your mom and I are getting a divorce."

Shannon had guessed that her dad was having an affair, but the news devastated her. She burst into tears. As soon as her dad hung up, Shannon called her mom, who hastily drove to the store and took her home.

Shannon's mom informed her of her father's words: "I don't love you. I like you; you are a nice person, but I am not *in* love with you, and I don't want to be married to you any longer." Shannon's parents divorced soon after.

Although she had recently become a born-again Christian, Shannon's mom spiraled downward. She had loved her husband deeply, but now she dumped her pain on Shannon, confiding in her daughter and telling her sordid stories of her husband's infidelities throughout the seventeen years of their marriage. Knowing her dad had been unfaithful to her mom was hard for Shannon to handle, but her mom's unwitting tendency to burden Shannon as her counselor exacerbated matters even further.

The infidelities caused Shannon to wonder, *Are all men going to cheat?*

To help ease the emotional pain, Shannon's mom began going out dancing at popular country music hot spots such as Gilly's, near Pasadena, Texas, often taking Shannon along with her. At the club, Shannon's mom allowed her sixteen-year-old daughter to drink alcoholic beverages and dance with older men.

Her dad married the woman for whom he had left Shannon's mom, and he began a new family, which caused Shannon's heart to ache even more. She felt as though she had been abandoned by her dad. Although still shy and almost reclusive, Shannon adopted the fashion trends of pop music star Madonna and embraced the artist's hit songs such as "Papa Don't Preach" and "Like a Virgin."

That's where Shannon was emotionally when we first met at church.

She had grown up attending a Catholic church but hadn't found the liturgy and ritual especially meaningful. Still, I did not lead her to Christ or influence her to convert from Catholicism to evangelical Christianity. She simply joined the youth group and realized on her own that she didn't have the kind of relationship with Jesus that we were talking about. Her grandmother had instilled in Shannon deep, biblically based values, so when she discovered that she could have a genuine relationship with the God of the Bible, she wanted it and committed her life to following Jesus. That made her even more attractive to me.

Not long after that, our youth leaders arranged for a bus to take a bunch of kids and young adults to a Christian concert at a local auditorium. Still trying to get her to like me, I sat right next to Shannon and her friend, Casey, a pretty girl with long brown hair. Shannon barely said a word. I interpreted Shannon's reluctance to talk as indifference, so I began talking and flirting with Casey. Shannon noticed. So when everyone stood up during a song, she purposely moved in between Casey and me, making the not-so-subtle point that she might be more interested in me than I had originally thought.

I smiled. To me, Shannon's jealousy was a good sign. Shannon and I sat together on the bus during the drive home. We dated and had fun together throughout the following year. Once we started dating, we were inseparable.

Both of us were going to high school and working part-time. We didn't have much spare time, and neither of us had much money, so most of our "dates" revolved around the church youth group activities. Our leaders, Steve and Melanie, thought we were a great couple. We went places and participated together with them, but they didn't try to push us.

Shannon's mom was attending church again, so she seemed to approve of us dating. She was a kind, sweet woman, with a passive sort of personality, so she may not have expressed opposition to our relationship anyhow. On the other hand, Shannon's dad, Bill, had remarried and was now living in Pittsburgh. He hated that his daughter was dating me and let her know it. Money meant a lot to him, especially as a signal that I could take care of his daughter. Since I didn't have a lot of money, that spoke volumes to Shannon's dad. Similar to the classic Buck Owens lyrics, "You don't know me, but you don't like me," Shannon's dad despised me, even though he didn't know me. Shannon's parents were already divorced when I met her. When Bill found out that I wanted to attend Bible school and was considering Jimmy Swaggart Bible College, he said, "They don't even have a football team!"

I saw Shannon's father infrequently. Shannon didn't speak much about him, except to occasionally mention that he used to make her feel inferior. "I knew my dad loved me," Shannon said years later, "but like many men of his generation, he had a different way of showing it." Perhaps because of his disciplined military background, in his attempts to bring out the best in her, Bill sometimes made insensitive comments such as, "Don't eat that. You're gonna get fat!" He'd quip, semiseriously, "You'll be a porker!" He seemed to assume that if he chided his daughter for wrong or unwise choices that she would make better ones. "Don't be stupid; do things right," he reminded her. Undoubtedly, he didn't realize how deeply his words seared into his daughter's heart and mind.

Although I didn't know it at the time, when Shannon would do silly things or hesitate about making a decision, if I made fun of her, my words, too, could hurt her deeply and lead her to feel worthless. I perpetuated her pain and didn't even realize it.

· · · · ·

While we were still seventeen, I told Shannon, "We're going to get married one day."

"You're out of your mind," she said with a laugh.

"No, we are," I said. "We're going to get married someday."

"Well, I don't see a ring," she quipped as she raised her left hand and perched her head to one side.

"Oh? You want a ring? Okay, fine, I'll get you a ring," I said, smiling broadly.

I talked with Steve Warriner about Shannon's comment, and he gave me the name of a friend who worked at a jewelry store. I went and bought a ring for Shannon. It was a thin, gold band with a half-carat diamond on a narrow Tiffany setting.

The next time we talked, I casually asked her, "If I did give you a ring, what kind would you like?"

"I really like rings with wide bands," she said.

Oh, no! I took the ring back to the jewelers and had them reset the diamond on a wide band.

On the day after Valentine's Day, Shannon and I participated in an all-night youth group "lock-in" at our church. During a break, while everyone else was outside in the church parking lot playing games, I pulled Shannon aside. I looked her in the eyes and said, "At some point, I want to marry you, and this is my proof." I took out the ring and placed it on Shannon's finger.

To our friends who saw the ring later that night, it was a promise ring. To Shannon and me, it was an engagement ring.

Since I had become a genuine Christian and not merely a church attender, I had learned more about the Bible and had discovered that God's Word restricted sex to within marriage. He wasn't depriving us; He wanted to protect us from emotional pain and physical disease that often accompany premarital or extramarital sex. He wanted to provide the best possible loving relationship in marriage. Consequently, I tried to restrain from sexual expressions with Shannon before marriage, as the Bible clearly taught. Shannon was more ambivalent about sex since she was a relatively new Christian and was just learning what the Scripture says about our bodies being a temple of the Holy Spirit. Granted, I was still a relatively new Christian as well, but I had grown up around biblical teachings—skewed though some might have been—all my life.

So although we struggled to keep the physical expressions of our love under control, our relationship didn't revolve around sex. We were best friends who fell in love with each other. On the other hand, we didn't buy into the hyper-Pentecostal type of relationship that prohibited even kissing each other before marriage. Truth is, we didn't feel deep convictions about abstaining from sex before marriage. Part of that had to do with our upbringings, part had to do with our declared intentions to marry, and part related to Shannon's and my lack of understanding about biblical teaching.

I took Shannon with me to Trinity, Texas, to meet my dad and Karen, my stepmom who was more like my own mother, and Karen's mother, who we called Granny. Just before our arrival, Granny had made some banana pudding.

"Do you want some banana pudding?" Granny asked Shannon sweetly.

"Sure!" Shannon said. Shannon loved banana pudding, and she watched with eyes sparkling as Granny loaded a bowl full of the stuff and handed it to her. And Shannon ate it!

Granny was delighted. "Would you like some more?" Granny asked.

"Ah, okay," Shannon hedged a bit, not quite as enthusiastic in her response this time yet still wanting to keep Granny happy. Shannon ate almost half of that bowl of banana pudding rather than say no to Granny and risk rejection.

She needn't have worried. My parents and Granny loved Shannon immediately and unconditionally. Although it would be severely tested, their love would turn out to be a tremendous blessing in the years ahead.

CHAPTER 7

NAIVE PREPARATIONS

I enrolled in Jimmy Swaggart Bible College, and Shannon accompanied my parents and me to Baton Rouge, where the school was located. After our tearful goodbyes, I plunged into learning how to be an evangelist. Shannon returned to Houston and continued working in the dental office during the first year of my academic studies. She saw herself as working in dentistry for the remainder of her life, perhaps as a dental hygienist.

I had given her a ring, indicating that we wanted to get married, but we had set no firm wedding date. We exchanged numerous letters, although Shannon wrote far more frequently than I did. She signed each card or letter "Shannon Michelle Pourteau," even though we weren't yet married. We talked by phone often, expressing our love to each other over and over with our conversations frequently colored by our heavy breathing.

As soon as I acclimated to campus life, I got busy, learning all that I could and getting involved in the ministry. I hosted a radio show at college on which I tried to imitate and preach like Jimmy Swaggart. Following his example, I spent most of my time preaching *against* sin rather than preaching *for* something, barely touching on foundational biblical topics such as forgiveness, grace, love, or redemption.

Nevertheless, I was popular on campus. I became friends with John Starnes, the copilot of Jimmy Swaggart's private jet. He was an incredible vocalist who also sang at Swaggart crusades. I got busy actively serving with Pastor Glen Burteau and the Crossfire youth group at the college church. Occasionally, I sang a solo at the Family Worship Center, Jimmy Swaggart's church, but I was not part of his crusade travel team. Although Brother Swaggart probably could have recognized me in a crowd, I'm not sure he ever really knew me by name.

The first time I sang for a Family Worship Center Sunday morning service, Jimmy Swaggart introduced me, "Ladies and gentleman, please welcome Jim *Porno*."

Oops! Most people didn't catch it, but I sure did, and the preacher's slip showed up again a few years later in his own life.

No doubt, his wife, Frances—the Ice Princess—as we students called her, noticed her husband's faux pas too. She hovered over every aspect of the ministry and ran it with an iron fist. She was not warmly embraced by most students. Christian television was booming at the time, though, and growing exponentially, so she continued to have tremendous influence. Her efforts were not in vain. Jimmy Swaggart was near the top of the heap when it came to television preachers.

I've never been a "go along to get along" sort of guy.

I was a good talker, popular, and a cocky nonconformist, even in Bible school. One of my professors (an old-school Hispanic charismatic) and I simply didn't hit it off. He didn't like me, and I didn't like him. He made us sing hymns a cappella before every class.

We were at Jimmy Swaggart Bible College where Jimmy Swaggart had sold millions of albums, so of course, every pastoral student needed to sing, but not in class. That seemed superfluous to me, and apparently the professor picked up on my attitude. Besides, I had a habit of spouting off in his class, voicing provocative or unpopular opinions or simply making a snippy remark intended to evoke an ill-timed laugh.

In the middle of class one day, the professor looked at me, turned to the chalkboard, and began drawing a large tree. Then he drew the ground and a line under the tree.

"James," he said. "This is you."

"What do you mean, Prof?"

In front of the entire class, he said, "Outside, above ground, everything is big and flowery and everyone says, 'Look at that tree. Isn't that amazing?' But underneath, your foundation is a tiny twig."

His words seared through me. I knew he was right, but his statements insulted me. He could have told me his insights privately rather than embarrassing me in front of my peers.

• • • • •

For the most part, though, I loved my classes at the college. I threw myself into studying the Bible, learning how to better present biblical truth, and was inspired by some truly great Christians. My evangelism professor, Dr. Paul Gibson, for example, was a tremendous soul winner and had a fabulous sense of humor. He truly cared about his students, and he cared even more about introducing people to Jesus. He boldly led a group of his students, including me, to attend Mardi Gras in New Orleans. He went there not to enjoy the festival but to "witness" to the rowdy crowds about how they could find true, lasting satisfaction in a relationship with Jesus. Some people jeered at him when he tried to share the gospel with them; others roughly shoved or shouldered him out of their way as the bawdy parade of inebriated, half-naked revelers surged down Bourbon Street. But the professor remained undeterred. I watched in admiration as Dr. Gibson knelt and prayed right on the pavement with more than a few folks who wanted to know how they could be saved.

My top desire, though, was to be like Jimmy Swaggart. I'd guess that many other Assemblies of God preachers did too.

Brother Swaggart was the cousin of the bombastic singer Jerry Lee Lewis, and evangelist Swaggart possessed a similar charisma and an incredible ability to emotionally move an audience. His passion for excellence in the entire crusade ministry—including his music, staging, and sound and lighting equipment—was unsurpassed. He was also controversial. I liked that about him. Ironically, he was against psychology and talked often about the demons of Christian counseling. He not only castigated Christian psychologists but also spiritually denigrated anyone who felt the need for their services, strongly implying that those Christians who sought help through psychology lacked true faith. He also seemed to hate most contemporary Christian music, especially music incorporating elements of rock and roll.

So that was the vision I had in front of me of what a Christian evangelist was supposed to be.

At one point during my first year of college, I tried to break up with Shannon. "This long-distance relationship is too hard," I told her. "You're living at home in Houston, and I'm here in Louisiana."

"Oh, no," Shannon said. "We're not breaking up." She got in her car and drove all the way to Baton Rouge to straighten me out. She wouldn't let me go!

Shannon hadn't grown up in Pentecostal churches as I had, so we thought it might be wise for us to learn together. We agreed that she should enroll at Jimmy Swaggart Bible College. Unfortunately, although she had been frugal with the money she earned as a dental assistant, it wasn't enough to pay for college.

Her dad refused to pay for her to attend school because he regarded her as an adult once she turned eighteen. Shannon recalls, "My dad's attitude was: Now that I was on my own, I should pay my own way for whatever I needed." But Bill may also have been less inclined to help her financially because she wanted to attend a Bible college rather than a liberal arts university. So *my* dad paid Shannon's tuition, housing, and other expenses, which amounted to several thousand dollars per semester.

I was enrolled in a two-year program, studying to earn an associate of arts degree in theology and pastoral counseling. Shannon enrolled in a one-year program for a Christian minister's certification, a program put together for a potential minister's wife. We enjoyed being in college together and, of course, being in close proximity to each other.

Shannon and I got along wonderfully in the early years of our relationship, although our personalities were quite different from each other. I was more outgoing. That worked well for us in some ways since I could let my gregarious side loose, and Shannon met a lot of new friends through me.

Although I hoped that Shannon would gain insight into what it meant to be a pastor's wife, I didn't expect her to be a "trophy wife" or a pretty ornament on my arm. That wasn't the case for many other young women at the Bible college. Sometimes it was referred to with an intentional slip of the tongue as the "Bridal College," since so many female students saw their futures as the wife of a pastor and hoped to secure an "MRS" degree. Later, Shannon commented, "Many of the women attending the Bible college were an active part of their husband's ministry, or they were planning to be. I was not. I didn't sing, teach, or play an instrument. I was not going to be a typical minister's wife."

And that was perfectly fine with me. I didn't appreciate the attitude expressed by some churches that when they hired a minister, it was a package deal and they received the minister's wife's services for free. I respected my fiancée too much to allow that to happen.

Despite her parents' difficult divorce, Shannon still thought in terms of the white picket fence images of family. She often babysat a little girl named Lindsey, so she planned to name her own daughter by that name if she were to have a baby girl. Thinking about us getting married and having children, Shannon concluded, "And because we are Christians, we will have the perfect little family."

No doubt, attending Jimmy Swaggart Bible College reinforced those images. "Surely, if my Jimmy is going to be in the ministry," Shannon said, "I won't ever have to worry about him cheating on me."

We were both incredibly naive.

CHAPTER 8

GUN SMOKE

While I was still at school, my dad's adopted brothers, Frank, Brett, and Donnie, contacted me. They had moved to Baton Rouge and now ran a vacuum company. They also handled bail bonds, pursuing people who had skipped court-appointed bail requirements. Oh, they also participated in and promoted professional wrestling—quite an eclectic bunch, my uncles were. One of them called and asked, "Hey, Jim, would you like to make some money?"

"Sure!"

"We could use some help with tracking down some bail bond people."

"Okay, cool."

I had purchased a .22 caliber pistol. There were no "conceal carry" laws at that time. Most of the kids I had grown up with carried guns in their trucks, but they had respect for the law and their fellow human beings. Interestingly, we never had a school shooting in our area.

I went to work with my uncles on weekends. But with about a month remaining in the spring semester, a kid in my dormitory found out that I had the gun, and he reported that I had a weapon on campus. In the middle of the night around one o'clock in the morning, the Christian college version of a SWAT team, including several administrators, burst into my room, searching everywhere.

"What are you looking for?" I asked groggily, rubbing the sleep from my eyes.

"Do you have a gun?" one of the intruders asked.

"Yes, I do," I said. I went over to the dresser and pulled out the .22 pistol. "Sometimes I work with my uncles doing bail bonds, so I need it to protect myself."

"Well, the college handbook says you cannot have a weapon on campus."

"Okay," I replied. It was late, I was sleepy, and I was trying to cooperate. Besides, I had nothing to hide. "But what if it is part of my job?"

"You still can't have it on campus."

"So what does that mean?" I asked.

"We'll have a student review. You violated school policy, so you'll have to appear before the disciplinary board, and they will decide."

When I went before the board, they told me, "We are going to recommend that you be expelled."

"Are you serious?" I asked. "You're going to kick me out of school and I haven't even violated the law, just a rule in the handbook that I wasn't even aware existed? You guys know me. I've been here for two years. You searched my room, and I didn't try to hide anything." I looked to one of the administrators. "I've eaten dinner with you!"

Another admin guy jumped in, pompously stating, "If you decide to withdraw, we will not expel you and you can keep your credits. This semester will file as an incomplete and you can return to school next semester. That is, if you are willing to go quietly and not make a scene."

They kicked me out of Bible school.

When I informed Shannon about the administration's decision, her bright eyes turned sullen. Confused and offended on my behalf, she asked, "Do you think I should leave too?"

"No, you stay and finish out the semester," I told her. "I'll figure this out."

I called my uncles and asked, "Can I come and live with you for a few days? These guys are booting me out of school."

"For what?" one of my uncles asked. "Did you get caught screwin' Shannon?"

"No, of course not," I said. "They found my gun that I use when we go out bounty hunting. It's a violation of the handbook, so they are suspending me."

"Well, hold on, I'm coming down there," Uncle Frank said.

A few days later, two of my uncles—massive, wrestler-looking types with long hair and beards and wearing cowboy boots—showed up on the campus of Jimmy Swaggart Bible College. Students, professors, and others audibly gasped as they saw the large, tattoo-covered men striding toward my dormitory. The expressions on their faces looked as though someone had just kicked their dog and they were on their way to "discuss" matters. My uncles had little respect for the school anyhow, so they were not concerned about offending anyone. "Where are the people that are giving you problems?" my Uncle Frank asked as soon as he saw me.

We went to the administration building and were quickly ushered into the dean's office, most likely so other people would not see the two unwelcome visitors. One uncle promptly propped his large cowboy boot right on the administrator's desk.

Oh, my! I thought. *This is not going to turn out well.*

A security guard—a student whose main job was to make sure other students weren't making out on campus—stopped by the door, looked in, and quickly assessed the scene. My uncle glared up at him and growled, "Son, for your own good, you might want to leave. Now."

The security guard found somewhere else to seek out student-lovers.

My uncles turned their attention to the dean. "We're gonna help Jimmy move, but first we want some explanations, and we won't leave till we get 'em. What's goin' on here?"

The dean told my uncles about the gun—information they already knew.

"So what you're telling me is that this boy is trying to become a minister," Frank said. "He's been studying hard and is livin' right and even has a little campus radio show. He's trying to earn some money working for me as a bail bondsman to help with his education, and you want to kick him out because he has a weapon. He didn't fire it or brandish it in front of anyone. You people just hear about it, and he gives it to you, and you still want to kick him out." Frank paused and leaned in toward the dean. "Explain this love of Jesus to me."

The dean was flustered and stumbled all over his words in trying to respond.

"Yeah," my uncle responded. "Exactly. You people and your kind are the reason I don't go to church anymore. Personally, I'm glad he's leaving here, because I think you all are a bunch of fakes."

The dean had no response. I sat quietly through it all. I had not known what my uncles were going to do prior to their appearance on campus, but I quietly withdrew from school, with full intention of returning the following fall term.

I left campus with my uncles. Shannon remained behind at school and finished out the semester, earning her certificate of ministry diploma. Then she returned home as well.

But by the time the following term rolled around, Brother Swaggart would be embroiled in a widely publicized scandal of his own, and I would never return to the school.

CHAPTER 9

LOUISIANA WEDDING

When Shannon came home from college in early May, she and I immediately began planning our wedding for November. We were so in love; we could hardly wait to be husband and wife.

The little church where we wanted to get married had a small parsonage that they were selling and wanted moved off their property. I prayed about it, and I felt that God instructed me to put in a bid for $1,000. That was a ridiculous amount to offer for a house, but two weeks later, my Pawpaw called and said, "Jimmy, they accepted your bid."

"For a thousand dollars?"

"Yep, it's all yours."

It cost me another $2,400 to have the house moved five miles to a piece of property I had purchased on a nearby swamp-surrounded island for about $2,000. So for under ten grand, and with some financial assistance from my dad and stepmom, we had a paid-off home of our own! That's where Shannon and I planned to set up housekeeping after our wedding. It just made sense for us to stay in Louisiana. My family was there, and I had some work potential with the local Emergency Medical Services team.

Most of Shannon's family was happy about our engagement and wedding plans. Shannon's dad, however, opposed our getting married so soon. "You're too young," he told Shannon. "And how is this preacher going to provide for you?" I wasn't offended. I understood that he loved his daughter and wanted the best for her—and on his ledgers, I didn't look like the best candidate.

He gave us $1,500 toward the wedding. "That's all I'll give you," he told his daughter.

Shannon found a woman who would make a wedding dress for $200, and it looked beautiful. The remainder of the money went toward transportation for Shannon's bridesmaids and $300 for some flowers for the church.

Thinking that we'd be returning to college for the winter session, we planned to get married on November 21, 1987 in the same church where my grandparents had publicly proclaimed their forever love. We were twenty years old and had received virtually no premarital counseling. My Uncle Buddy did give me some of his usual sage advice. He told me, "You don't have to wear her out the first night." With that sort of wisdom, how could we go wrong?

About seventy-five to a hundred people attended our wedding. The ceremony was scheduled to begin at 3:00 p.m., but when the wedding processional began, there were still no flowers at the church. The flower lady—a relative—showed up late without any flowers, so there were no additional decorations in the sanctuary, except some hurriedly placed faux ivy strung over a sort of standing arch at the front. Brother Mann, the pastor of the church, and Brother Rene Salzman, the former pastor of that church for more than forty years from the time my grandparents first began attending there to when I was a kid, shared in officiating the relatively short ceremony.

I was getting nervous before the wedding, so my pawpaw handed me a small, white tablet. "Here, take this," he said.

"What is it?" I asked.

"Never you mind," he said with a grin. "It's a Valium. Just take it. It will calm you down." Pawpaw had a Valium prescription for his heart problems, at least so he said, so he always carried some with him.

"I don't need to calm down," I said. "I'm getting married. I'll pass out from that thing."

"Oh, just take it," Pawpaw said with a shrug.

So I did. The tranquilizer did calm me, but I was half-loopy throughout most of the wedding ceremony.

Despite the many broken vows, divorces, and remarriages, our parents all showed up at our wedding.

Shannon's dad attended the wedding, although he may have hoped an intervention was still possible. At the back of the church, just prior to walking the bride down the aisle, he leaned over to Shannon and said, "It's not too late. If you turn around now and don't get married, I'll buy you a brand new car."

Shannon looked back at him, her eyes wide, surprised by her dad's suggestion. "No, Dad. I want to get married!"

She continued walking the remainder of the aisle.

Shannon later joked, "I should have said, 'Okay, I'll take the car,' and then we could have eloped in a brand new car!"

During our wedding, we said "I do" and made some serious vows to each other. I sang to Shannon the song, "A Household of Faith," first popularized by Christian music artist Steve Green. The lyrics describe how we intended to build a household founded on faith in Jesus Christ, "and together we will stand." It was an emotional moment in an already audacious and overwhelming day.

Following the service, we went to a fellowship hall behind the main church for the reception, where folks snacked on cake and punch and some finger foods. We couldn't afford anything else, and most of the food was homemade and donated by some of the women in the family and church.

Since we had little money of our own, my parents gifted us with a four-day trip to Puerto Vallarta, Mexico, for our honeymoon.

We returned to Houston and stayed at Shannon's mom's home to celebrate our first Thanksgiving together as a married couple. That weekend, we drove back to our new home in Louisiana.

Shannon and I were like two starry-eyed little kids, excited about our new life together. We loved each other dearly and set up housekeeping in our thousand-dollar house.

The house was tiny and old, with ugly, green shag carpet, but it was ours. We had a screened-in porch we used as a laundry room. We had a small room off the living room that Shannon and I used as an office. We warmed the house with propane heaters mounted on the wall. Two large air-conditioning units hung in the windows, and when the AC was on high, the noise was so loud it was nearly impossible to have a conversation in the house.

We lived on the swamp-surrounded island in Big Lake, Louisiana. I worked as an EMS with the fire department in Lake Charles, and Shannon worked in an orthodontist's office.

I still wanted to be an evangelist. My perpetual cheerleader, Shannon said, "Let's go. I love to travel." We had no clue what the evangelist's life entailed apart from what we had seen from some of the popular television ministers, most notably Jimmy Swaggart.

Although she was relatively new to the faith, Shannon was good at explaining basic Christianity to people, showing them that it was more about a personal relationship with Jesus rather than religion and more a matter of the heart instead of mere external rituals.

We had few close friends in Big Lake, though we attended the nondenominational church where my extended family members had attended for generations and where we had gotten married. Despite Shannon's Catholic background, she was comfortable with the more charismatic expressions during the worship services.

I taught a few Bible classes, sang solos, and helped with the music program at the church.

The church's attitude toward women was quite traditional, with no women preachers, although several women in the congregation served as highly respected Sunday school teachers. Shannon didn't want to do those things anyhow. She enjoyed helping with the children's ministries, assisting with the church social events, and serving in other practical ways. The women dressed plainly and conservatively and looked quite "country" since the church was on their island.

· · · · ·

In the early days of our marriage, Shannon avoided conflict at all costs. That frustrated me. I didn't feel she was being honest with me. At times when we were discussing some complicated topic, I might ask her, "Do you understand?"

"Uh-huh," she replied, simply wanting to keep the peace.

But if I pressed her, she'd come clean. "You don't really understand a thing I just said, do you?" I asked.

"Well, no, not really. But it's okay."

"No, Shannon, it is not okay. Don't you realize that you are lying to me? I would much rather you say, 'No, Jim, I don't have a clue,' and then I could explain or we could discuss it. But when you placate me and act like you know, it causes me to disrespect you. If you say you don't understand, we can talk about that."

But Shannon's background was to keep the peace, even if it meant denying her own opinions or values. Even if she was disconcerted or discontent, her attitude was "I'd rather keep that inside and deal with it internally."

Of course, I didn't know that on our wedding day. She was attractive, easy to get along with, a fun companion, and spiritually devout, so the fact that we had no intellectual conversations didn't seem to matter. I'd later discover that it did. That led to Shannon feeling dumb, and I didn't help. "What are you? Stupid or something?" I sometimes railed when she misunderstood me. She couldn't win. I got mad when she pretended to understand a concept I wanted to get across to her, and I mocked her when she couldn't catch it.

I didn't know that her dad had used similar derisive language to denigrate Shannon as a little girl. Years later when I realized that I had damaged her in the same way, I grieved over my insolence and I apologized to her.

I knew that I loved her and that she loved me. That's all that mattered—or so we thought.

PART III

THIS WOULDN'T
HAPPEN TO US

CHAPTER 10

How Could This Happen?

February 1988: "I have sinned!" Those words may have encapsulated the most broadly heard confession since the biblical characters of Saul, King David, or Judas, whose mistakes we can now read about in Scripture. But when Jimmy Swaggart uttered those words on television, tears mixed with perspiration running down his face, millions of people watched the telecast and either wept with him or made fun of him.

Shannon and I were in our bedroom one evening when we saw the news coverage regarding my spiritual hero visiting prostitutes. My wife and I literally wept as the sordid details of Jimmy Swaggart's illicit activities became public. My whole life was wrapped up with going to his school to study for the ministry, so his moral failures disappointed Shannon and me deeply.

Moreover, Swaggart's public scandal made it even harder for Shannon's family to accept my family and me. They didn't understand it all, but they associated us with the fallen evangelical leader. "That's what you are—those kind of people?" they asked Shannon.

It was so disheartening to see the popular minister's failures splashed all over television, newspapers, and magazines. There was no social media back then, and thankfully so.

How could such a thing happen? We both wondered and asked repeatedly. We were glad that we were not at school when everything came down. Shannon and I knew we would most likely not return to college at Jimmy Swaggart Bible College, so we resigned ourselves to living near my childhood home in Louisiana. I was preaching occasionally and had a few potential invitations waiting.

Scandals were nothing new. Certainly, political and business moguls had recently been in the news for all sorts of moral indiscretions, everything from sexual affairs to bilking stockholders out of billions of dollars. But we had always assumed that most ministers, while not immune from temptation, held themselves to a higher standard and at least attempted to live as role models.

Now, suddenly, it seemed the lid had been blown off Pandora's box.

It was a tumultuous time in Christian ministries. Jim Bakker had left PTL with Heritage USA under a cloud of sexual and financial scandal in January 1987. Marvin Gorman, pastor of a Louisiana megachurch, admitted to having an affair; he had been outed by Jimmy Swaggart. In turn, Reverend Gorman had exposed the immoral activities of Jimmy Swaggart, which was followed by Swaggart's debacle. What a mess.

Shannon and I didn't hear a word from anybody at school after we left Jimmy Swaggart Bible College. Not a word.

• • • • •

I was already preaching evangelistic services in small churches in Louisiana, so I accepted invitations if and when they came. Few did.

I could preach strong messages and persuade people, but I had no desire to manipulate a congregation to get a response to the message, to me, or even to God. That was the Spirit's responsibility, not mine. I was the messenger, that's all.

I wanted to keep the gospel message simple and uncomplicated, devoid of religious jargon, and not bogged down by a particular denomination's doctrine. Consequently, I preached more about the love of God, and I didn't preach hellfire and brimstone any longer. That freed me to love people wherever they were, despite their lifestyles. I told them, "There is a God who gave His Son for you so you can really live. You need to meet Him." I wanted people who already knew Christ to grow stronger in their faith, not merely sit in church for an hour or so each week. I caught a lot of flak from other Assemblies of God pastors who thought I was watering down the message.

Although I never returned to Jimmy Swaggart Bible College, I was grateful for what I had learned there. Besides the emphasis on doing things with excellence, I learned from a "Who's Who" of Christian leaders as the school hosted a parade of guest speakers, many of whom were godly role models and world changers. They didn't merely talk about taking the gospel to the world; they were *doing* it, and some had done it for years. So despite Brother Swaggart's highly publicized fall, I left school built up in my faith rather than disillusioned.

I have always been good in tense situations and making difficult decisions. Since I had so few preaching opportunities, I started looking for another way to support Shannon and me. Our family ranks included some police officers. So I worked with them for a while, but I enjoyed the medical side more, so I went back to school and earned a paramedic's license. I worked for the ambulance company as a medical technician and with the police department at the same time. Meanwhile, Shannon was working as a receptionist to help us make ends meet.

Despite the pall cast over the spiritual role of evangelists, I felt strongly that I should be one, presenting the gospel and helping to dispel people's doubts. I never really wanted to be a pastor because I didn't feel that I had enough patience for that sort of service. I could preach a strong message, and I was deeply concerned, compassionate, and caring, but I was not willing to coddle people. "We're all here to serve God and each other," I told our congregation. "It isn't a pastoral show; each of us is important and has a job to do."

In Pentecostal churches, we often judged someone's spirituality by their do and don't lists. Now, I came to evaluate people by their service.

I was still part of our church denomination and then went back to school several years later through remote learning at Louisiana Baptist University to study counseling and psychology. The school accepted some of my credits from Bible college, so I didn't feel that my time at Jimmy Swaggart Bible College had reaped no educational benefit.

Shannon and I were living about twenty miles out of Lake Charles and struggling to make ends meet. I didn't know how to manage our finances or how real life functioned, so not surprisingly, I put us in debt quickly. My mom had given me an American Express credit card when I was only seventeen so I could buy gas to get to work. Now, as a newly married homeowner, with about one acre of grass to mow, I decided I needed a new lawn mower. I went to a department store to purchase a riding mower, and the store was "kind enough" to grant me one of their credit cards. Then I got another one. Before long, I had plunged us deeply into debt. We barely scraped by each month, struggling hard to stay ahead of our creditors.

Still, we were happy. We had family nearby and felt that our future was secure.

During those first years of our marriage, Shannon and I experienced misunderstandings similar to many couples as we adjusted our unrealistic expectations to real life. Sometimes our arguments exploded into full-blown fights, but neither of us felt any inclination to walk away from our marriage. As far as we were concerned, we were in it for the long haul, and, with enough love and patience, we would work through any misunderstandings—eventually.

• • • • •

While working with the ambulance team, I occasionally received an invitation to speak at a church, and I almost always accepted. I enjoyed preaching and still hoped to be "the next Jimmy Swaggart," minus the scandal. Shannon and I were active in our church community, and I taught some classes there for about a year.

I received a call from Mike Lofton, who pastored the Church of God in Trinity, Texas. Mike knew my dad and me. "I'm looking for an associate and a youth pastor," he said, "and we'd love to have you here."

"Really? You want *me*?" I asked.

"Absolutely," Pastor Mike responded. "I've heard good things about you. Are you interested?"

"Well, yeah!" I nearly yelled into the phone. "Let me talk with Shannon, and I'll call you right back."

Shannon and I briefly discussed the opportunity, and we both felt we were ready for a change.

I couldn't wait to accept Pastor Mike's offer. Finally, I could preach and still make a living, two concepts that weren't always compatible at many small churches in our circles.

Shannon and I moved to Texas to serve the congregation of a couple hundred people. The church was a typical Pentecostal, "Holy Roller" sort of environment, and Pastor Mike modeled a genuine love for the people. Mike was a big old boy who'd walk up to a rancher in a field, look him in the eye, and say, "Hey, man! I love you. I just want you to know I'm here for you."

I had never before seen or heard anyone do that—at least not a man's man saying "I love you" to another man or to someone to whom he wasn't related. But Mike truly loved people, and I adopted many of his simple expressions of true Christianity.

I also learned some bad habits while at the church, including appeasing people and avoiding conflict. Mike loved his congregation and wanted to keep them happy, so he avoided confronting issues head-on. Since he was a positive role model in my life, I wanted to be like, look like, and sound like Mike.

I was satisfied and content serving the congregation in Texas when I received a phone call from Mark Evans, a pastor at New Life Assemblies of God church, a congregation of about five hundred people in Trumbull, Connecticut, near Bridgeport. I had spent several months there leading a street evangelism team a few years earlier. Our approach had been to take a video camera out along the streets of Bridgeport and ask people about God, their opinions on how to get to heaven, and other questions about their beliefs. We discovered that many people we interviewed weren't sure of their answers, so we invited them to church. Others we introduced to Jesus right there on the streets. In an area of New England known to be rather spiritually "dry," our no-pressure evangelistic efforts were highly effective.

Mark was aware of all that, but that was not the primary reason he called. "Hey, Jim, we're looking for a youth pastor," he said.

"Oh, that's great. Maybe I can help you find someone," I offered. "What sort of person are you looking for?"

"Well, actually, we're looking for someone exactly like you," Mark replied.

"Oh," I said, as the implications of Mark's words hit me. "Well, Mark, I'm pretty happy right here where I am," I said. "I love it. It's Texas, the people are friendly, and it feels like home."

Trinity, Texas, and Bridgeport, Connecticut, seemed like worlds apart to me, and they were.

Nevertheless, Pastor Mark invited me to visit and interview with his team, so I talked to Mike Lofton about it. "I'm not really interested in leaving," I told Mike, "but this church has called and asked me to consider being their youth pastor. What do you think?"

Mike looked back at me and wrinkled his cheek a bit. "Hmm," he said, rubbing his chin as though thinking how to answer best.

"Well, I wouldn't want to lose you," Mike said in his slow Texas drawl, "but I don't think you should shut the door on a ministry opportunity without checking it out, especially when there are no red flags." Mike wasn't possessive of me, nor was he attempting to push me away.

I was somewhat surprised at Mike's gracious response but deeply appreciative of his willingness to be open to what was best for me and for the congregation in Connecticut.

Shannon and I visited with the pastors and congregation in Trumbull. The church was associated with the Assemblies of God denomination. Mark's father, Reverend Don J. Evans, had come to America from Wales, preaching as an evangelist for a series of revival services. Formerly convicted as a safecracker who had served time in prison in Wales, Don Evans was now a powerful proponent of Christianity. A man of great faith, he felt that God told him to sell his return ticket, so he did. Rather than returning home, he stayed in the United States and founded the congregation in Trumbull, starting from scratch and building a thriving spiritual community of around five hundred members by the time I first visited. Eventually, the church grew to more than thirteen hundred members, but the leadership remained a family affair. Don's son, Mark—about ten years my senior—served as the associate pastor. He and his wife, Debbie, were friends of mine. Jason Evans, Mark's younger brother, was also on the staff, working with music and graphics.

Mark was a balding, portly guy with a flamboyant flair; he was hard to miss. Although he had no formal theological education, he was a bright man who knew how to influence people. He had been friends with Jimmy Swaggart's son, so Mark and his dad, Don, had rushed to assist the Swaggarts in handling the scandal following Brother Swaggart's fall. I appreciated their willingness to plunge into the swirling waters of unpopular public opinion. At the time, I saw that as a plus.

When I talked to Shannon about the possibility of moving to Connecticut, she was ambivalent but supportive. "I just want to go with you," she said. "I want to be wherever you want to be." Although I appreciated her cooperative, altruistic spirit, it was of little help regarding whether I should accept the position in Connecticut.

Nevertheless, after briefly considering my options, I accepted the position as youth pastor of New Life Assemblies of God church. We went back home to inform Mike and begin planning for the transition. Four months later, in September 1992, we headed for New England.

CHOICES HAVE
CONSEQUENCES

Once in Trumbull, I hit the ground running and poured myself into building the church's youth program. At our first meeting, only seven kids showed up from a congregation of nearly five hundred people. Not exactly a stellar turnout. Clearly, we had a lot of room to grow, and I had a lot to learn.

Our first year there was awkward. Raised in the southern part of the United States and coming to Trumbull from Trinity, I ran smack into the differences between life in warm, friendly, open-armed Texas and the chilly, reserved, less emotional atmosphere in New England. Talk about culture shock. I experienced it full force.

Making my transition even more tenuous, the Evans family members were quite British in their formal attitudes, demeanor, and lifestyles. One day I needed something from Pastor Don. He and his wife, June, lived a short walk down a hill from the church, so I simply went to their house and knocked on the front door.

Pastor Don opened the door and stared at me. "James?" he said quizzically. He looked like a chunkier version of Sean Connery with a slightly balding head and an immaculately trimmed, white goatee beard. As always, he was dressed impeccably, even at home.

"Hey, Pastor," I greeted him amicably. "I was just curious; I was looking for something. . . ."

The pastor interrupted me. "James, what are you doing here?"

"Well, I was looking for. . . ."

Pastor Don waved his hand in front of his face. "James, you must call before you come to our home." With that he shut the door.

He wasn't being mean. He was merely formal and proper about British manners. He maintained clear boundaries and apparently expected me to do the same. That was new to me, coming from Texas where Mike and I functioned as brothers.

Pastor Don also operated under the leadership mentality of "Never let them see you sweat," or, more likely, Pastor Don would say, "Never let them see you *perspire*." His attitude was always, "You must maintain an edge—a barrier—between you and the congregation or they won't respect you."

The Evans family spoke "Christianese" much more fluently than I did, using formal language and a lot of flowery phrases. In their sermons, they often quoted famous, dead preachers, such as Charles Spurgeon, Charles Finney, and others. Their approach worked well in New England.

But it wasn't me.

I never talked down to the kids; I spoke to them straightforwardly. I treated them just as I would adults, with respect, dignity, and a willingness to listen sincerely to what they were thinking or was of concern to them. The kids responded positively and invited their friends to attend youth gatherings. Before long, we had more than one hundred and fifty guys and girls in our group. The church purchased an old bus so we could drive into Bridgeport on Friday nights and pick up more kids who had no transportation. Each week, we filled the bus with kids, took them back to Trumbull for youth services and activities, and then took them back to Bridgeport.

I recruited help from the congregation and soon had at least thirty adults on our volunteer youth staff. We developed a summer youth camp for five hundred kids from churches in our district. I preached youth messages but also spoke to other groups almost every week. The pastors and other church leaders approved of our efforts wholeheartedly and seemed greatly pleased at our success. Occasionally, I did some preaching to the congregation. I grew to a place where the only programs in which I did not get involved were those regarding women and young children. "That's because I've never understood either one of them!" I said with a laugh.

Perhaps reflecting Pastor Don's personality, the Sunday morning services at New Life were rather structured, especially for a charismatic congregation. Exuberant expressions, spoken prophecies, or messages in tongues were rare, unless they emanated from the pastor or his family members. I was fine with that. I had been filled with the Holy Spirit and thoroughly entrenched in Pentecostal thinking. I had even spoken in tongues—considered by many in our denomination as the initial evidence of a deeper relationship with God. As I studied the Bible, however, I was convinced from the apostle Paul's teachings that the gifts of the Spirit are disseminated as *He* chooses and that as believers, we don't all have the same gifts. We are a part of the same body, but each person has his or her own gift or gifts given by the Spirit. So I was comfortable with the less effusive approach to such expressions at New Life.

The Evans family became our extended family. Once I learned how they operated, we got along fantastically well. We enjoyed being around them and even vacationed together. Jason Evans and I became super close friends, and I served with him on the worship team. We sang a lot of Jimmy Swaggart songs, so it was a natural fit for me.

When the choir director left, I stepped up and took on those responsibilities. We performed nearly every Sunday morning and presented two full cantatas or other musicals each year. Additionally, I received an invitation from Christian Heritage School, a highly regarded private prep school in Trumbull, to teach a New Testament survey class to their junior high students and help with their junior high girls basketball team.

"Sure, I would love to do that," I said. I accepted the invitation and taught at the school for more than eight years. I also coached the junior high boys basketball team. In all that, I never missed a beat with our youth program. Our church had the largest youth group in the area.

There were no women pastors on our staff. Nor did we invite many female guest speakers. The leaders of the church had mostly come out of ultraconservative backgrounds, so they were simply perpetuating what they had learned, which resulted in a more patriarchal hierarchy of leadership.

That was okay with us. Shannon felt no compulsion to scratch and claw her way up the ministerial ladder to success. She just wanted to be a good wife and in the future a great mom. Even when we discovered that our chances of having children naturally were slim, she was undeterred.

We explored artificial insemination programs and found a good one at Yale University Hospital. We did a first in vitro treatment at Yale once we were settled in Connecticut. Shannon was a trooper. She really disliked receiving shots. Even when we had done the blood tests before our wedding, she had nearly passed out. But for the in vitro treatment, Shannon willingly endured a shot every day for months because she wanted to have a baby. Sadly, the treatment did not work for us.

We got pregnant three times, however, even without the help of the in vitro treatments, but in both of the first two pregnancies, when Shannon was about six weeks along, we lost the babies. Prior to the third miscarriage, Shannon was unaware she was even pregnant. She had been visiting her dad when she began experiencing a great deal of pain in her side. When she returned home, she did a pregnancy test, and it was positive. But when her doctors examined her, they discovered her pain was the result of a tubal pregnancy, a potentially life-threatening situation for her. She was admitted to the hospital and miscarried for the third time.

Shannon's heart was broken, but that same night, we attended a birthday party for some of our friends' children. In the days and weeks following the miscarriage, we cried together and apologized to each other profusely for our failure to have a child. After a while, I said, "We have to stop this. It is no one's fault. We've done all we can do."

Shannon and I believed that God is in charge, and having a baby was up to Him. We took the medical steps. The rest was His doing. Or not.

The doctors could find no physical reason why we could not have a baby. That was puzzling and frustrating. Shannon had grown up with a large extended family, so she really wanted to have children of our own. I was more ambivalent. It wasn't to be, despite all our prayers.

Shannon and I didn't follow a traditional prayer routine about our infertility or other concerns. Sure, we both prayed, but we never established a set daily prayer time and didn't often pray together. It simply wasn't convenient because of our schedules. I had grown up in an environment where lack of prayer was a horrific sin. Shannon had only loosely followed the requirements of Catholicism, so we didn't function in any particular pattern of prayer. Moreover, my idea of prayer was not sitting down together for thirty minutes and going over a list, whether they were real needs or a Christmas list of requests expressed to God. My habit has always been to talk with

God all through the day as thoughts pop into my mind. I ask questions, sometimes I gripe and complain, but always in the course of a natural conversation with God. I don't use fancy words or take on a profoundly "spiritual" sounding voice as I pray. I simply talk with God.

As far as Bible study, I might read portions of the Bible on any given day, or I may read a devotional or meditation type of book that helps me focus on the joy of the Lord. I refused to allow my spiritual input to become ritualistic or a badge showing how strong of a Christian I was. For me, prayer and meditation on God went together. I wanted to hear from Him, not merely hear myself talk.

Shannon and I did both pray, especially about having children. But we also believed that God was sovereign, so we never shook our fists in His face, complaining, "God, why are You holding out on us?"

We didn't give up on the hope of having children; we even considered the possibility of adopting a child. Every state in the Union has children who need a "forever home," and it has often been pointed out that if a family in every church in America would each provide a home for just one child, the state-run foster care programs would become unnecessary.

We initiated the process of adoption, but shortly into the program, we decided it wasn't for us. We accepted the fact that we might never be parents, but we had children to influence through the youth ministry. We had teenagers at our home almost constantly. We didn't blame God or hold any residual anger in our hearts. He was in charge, and in areas over which He gave me control, I knew that He gave me freedom. I made those choices, so I also had to accept the consequences. That was a lesson I would learn again and again the hard way.

CHAPTER 12

YOUTHFUL ENERGY

S hannon and I settled down in Trumbull, Connecticut, and I continued working with the church for the next sixteen years. We loved the people in our congregation and especially enjoyed working with the teens and young adults. We envisioned ourselves living there for the remainder of our lives—and we were barely in our thirties!

Having acclimated to the New England culture, we formed many great friendships with the people of the congregation. One of the closest relationships we developed was with Micah and Charlotte, a husband and wife about our age. Micah and Charlotte were super active in the church, and we worked together in the ministry, so we saw each other regularly and soon discovered we had many things in common. We loved the same sorts of music, movies, and sports, and we shared many deeply meaningful conversations. We cooked out at their house or ours almost every weekend, and occasionally we vacationed together as well. To me, Micah and Charlotte were family—in some ways they were even closer than family.

We spoke honestly together about our innermost thoughts or feelings, our hopes and dreams, our successes and failures, and our vulnerabilities. Never one to be too open with anyone other than Shannon, I found myself trusting Micah and Charlotte more than anyone in our world. I just knew that they would never betray my confidence or compromise our friendship in any way. We were "family."

· · · · ·

Our church was located in Fairfield County, one of the richest in the nation; many men and women dressed quite fashionably. On the other hand, many of the kids we picked up in our church bus and brought to youth group activities were street kids whose parents did not attend our church. Many were Black or Puerto Rican kids. Some of them had not worn clean clothes in ages and most had not eaten that day if a free breakfast or lunch program wasn't available at the school.

My own rejection and fear of abandonment growing up created an affinity for these poor, disenfranchised kids. I knew they would not spontaneously come to us, so we devised various ways of taking the gospel message to them. One of the best things we did was buying that old bus and going into Bridgeport to bring them to the church. A few folks in our congregation balked at bringing poor, disheveled kids, many of whom had serious physical or emotional problems, into our pristine, predominantly White Anglo-Saxon Protestant church. But Shannon and I loved those kids, and they loved us back. Although our time in Connecticut was awkward at first as we made the transition from Texas, our Puerto Rican and Black friends helped us with a part of life they knew: not being accepted initially.

We had so many underprivileged kids coming to youth group on Friday nights, we started an Upward Sports basketball league. Most of these kids would never have the chance to play ball for some of the upscale schools around our area, but they could play ball at the church—for free. Kids came from all over the area, and we soon had about six hundred kids playing basketball together every week. I worked hard to recruit coaches and assistants who would not only help the kids learn to play basketball but also learn good life lessons. We gathered a dedicated group of young men and a few athletically talented women who were willing to work with the young kids every week. The kids loved playing basketball, and during halftime or after the games, we had opportunities to tell them about Jesus.

The officials for the games, however, were terrible. Besides a lack of ability, they simply were not consistent. One call would seem too picky, another too lenient. I was always frustrated over the referees, so I went to officials' school and tested to be a referee myself. I discovered that I really enjoyed being a basketball referee. Before long, I began officiating high school and even college basketball games. It gave me a fantastic opportunity to serve and meet needs. And the exercise was pretty demanding too.

Shannon and I were practically surrogate parents to hundreds of kids in the youth group. We allowed them to hang out with us, and we went where the kids were—to their games, concerts, recitals, anywhere. We also let it be known that our home was open to the kids day or night, and many of them showed up. In addition, Shannon and I hosted our youth leadership team of about eighteen kids, male and female, at our house every Friday night for a number of years. An adjunct group to the church youth program, these mostly older teens were really the ones who helped lead the program. We transformed our basement into an arcade, complete with a big screen television, video games, a pool table, and other games. Kids came to our house frequently. We loved having them, and they often commented that they enjoyed hanging out with us.

Their presence was a double blessing for us. After trying so hard for so long to have a baby of our own, God had given us more kids than we could have imagined having in our home!

• • • • •

Not all of the kids attracted to our church youth group were easy targets for spiritual transformation. A tough-looking Puerto Rican dude nicknamed Birdman came to our youth service every week. He was sixteen or seventeen, and we knew he was a drug dealer.

Some people in our church asked me occasionally, "Are you worried about going into the inner city to reach kids?" They were concerned about the violence and crime, and indeed, I had to confiscate a gun from a kid on our church bus on one occasion.

"Naw," I said with a grin. "One of the biggest drug dealers in town is in our youth group."

Birdman came with his girlfriend and brought his brothers and sisters to youth meetings every week. Shannon and I loved him. He was always respectful of her and called her Miss Shannon. After months of building a relationship, Shannon said to him one evening, "I love you, Birdman."

"I love you, too, Miss Shannon," he said without a moment's hesitation. "I appreciate all you do for my brothers and sisters. They need to hear this."

"What about you, man?" I asked.

"It's too late for me," he said sadly. "I've already made my choices. I know what I have to do."

He nodded toward his brothers and sisters. "But they need to hear it."

It really broke our hearts that Birdman had become convinced that he would die without faith, that it was too late for him to change his life. I believed then, and still do, that it is never too late to start doing the right thing and making positive changes in our lives, especially when God is involved. But without hope that circumstances can change and life can be better, it is almost impossible to experience lasting transformation. As I told the kids, "If you don't know where you want to go, any road will take you there."

We didn't give up on Birdman and continually hoped that he might step across that spiritual dividing line and trust Jesus for himself. He never did while I was in Trumbull, but I still loved him and prayed that one day he would.

• • • • •

Our youth group was active on the local level with exciting activities, but one of the most important things I wanted them to learn was how to serve. So we took more than fifty of our teenagers on two mission trips to Venezuela. Some families of the teenagers and other members in the church gave up their vacations to accompany us. A few of the children who went were only nine years old and on their very first mission trip. Imagine the effect such a trip could have on a child from an affluent American family who plays basketball in an impoverished country with another child around the same age who cannot speak English and barely has enough food to eat or clothes to wear. That sort of experience can change a person's worldview for life.

Before going on this trip, I had met Gary, a missionary friend, and told him that I was looking for a place to go where we could do nontraditional mission trips. Gary told me about the needs in Venezuela. We went and worked with the people, held basketball camps with the kids, helped construct a church, and, yes, had some church services with them too. Mostly we went to Venezuela to share our hope in Jesus Christ, and as a result, a large number of the Venezuelans we served decided to trust Jesus.

When we concluded one of our trips to Venezuela, the Chavez government authorities, who were strongly anti-American at the time, wouldn't let our entire group board the plane to return to the United States. Only about thirty of our group were permitted to board our flight, but then the gate agent said, "No mas! No more."

"What do you mean we can't get everyone on board?" I protested.

"No mas," she said and walked away.

It was a nightmare trying to figure out where everyone in our group was, who was on the plane, and who was not. In several cases, parents and their children were separated. I immediately set about trying to contact parents back home, letting them know about the problem, that only part of our group was aboard the first flight, and the remainder of our troupe was safe and hoped to return soon. Finally, after two more days, the authorities allowed us to rebook our flights from Caracas to Miami. In the meantime, Gary helped me to obtain hotel rooms for our group and to make all the arrangements. Eventually we got everyone home, but we learned how vulnerable and defenseless we were in a foreign country.

On one mission trip to Vera Cruz, Mexico, we worked with a group of impoverished kids known as "the forgotten people" because they lived in the garbage dumps, scavenging for any remnants of food they could find. Our hosts warned us before we arrived at the dumps, "Stay on the plastic that we lay on the dirt. There are parasites in the dirt, and if you touch the dirt and then touch your face, you could pick up deadly bacteria." We spent the day ministering to the kids in the dumps. The local kids were so excited to see our group that they were literally hanging off shanty roofs so they could watch and hear the American "gringos" telling them about Jesus.

As we were riding back to the mission site in our bus, we were talking and singing after a rewarding day's work. I sat in the front of the bus, casually talking with the bus driver, when suddenly, from out of the weeds, came a guy on his bicycle heading across the road directly in front of us. The driver slammed on the brakes and swerved to miss him, but he was too late. Traveling at thirty miles per hour or more, the bus smacked right into the bike rider.

Startled by the dull thud of the impact, my paramedic's training kicked in nonetheless. "Oh, my gosh! We hit somebody!" I yelled. The driver pulled the bus to the side of the road, and I quickly turned to the thirty or more kids and adults on our bus. "Everybody stay inside the bus," I ordered. "Mary, you come with me."

Mary, who spoke fluent Spanish, hurried off the bus along with me to treat the bike rider. We looked in front of the bus and found the crushed bicycle caught in the front bumper, but we couldn't find the man. We found the shoes he had been wearing but nothing more. He had disappeared and was nowhere to be found. I looked under the bus and could hardly believe my eyes. A man's body was caught in the wheel well of the bus's front left tire!

I gently moved the man's shoulder and eased him out from under the bus and onto the ground, each move accompanied by his agonizing, painful wails. I laid him flat on his back and raised his feet up, talking to him in English with Mary translating. I glanced up and noticed that a crowd of Mexican locals was quickly gathering.

Our missionary host came to Mary and me and said, "We have to leave."

"What do you mean, leave?" I asked. "I'm trying to help this guy."

"No, the police will get here soon. They are already on their way, I promise you," the missionary said. "They are going to get here and see thirty or more Americans in a bus, and they won't understand what happened, so they will arrest all of us and take us to jail, and then they will try to sort it out tomorrow. You and the bus riders will have to leave. Now."

I tried to make the injured man as comfortable as possible. Then I stepped onto the bus to give instructions to our team members. "Hurry," I said. "We are going to leave the bus and driver and our missionary here, so we are going to have to walk the rest of the way back."

We hurriedly exited the bus and started running down the back roads. It was ludicrous. There we were, a bunch of Americans all dressed in matching bright yellow T-shirts, trying to look inconspicuous as we attempted to evade the police. Who were we kidding? They could have seen us from outer space!

When we finally felt that we were safe, I gathered the kids and adults together. "Okay," I told them, "whatever the enemy means for evil, God can use for good. Let's just pray." So that's what we did. "God, please work this out. Please help the injured man be okay. And please don't let our driver get arrested. Bring good out of this situation."

That night, our group took part in an evangelistic crusade in Vera Cruz. When I saw our missionary host, I asked, "How's the guy who we hit?"

"He's here!" the local missionary exuded.

"What?"

"Yes, we stayed with him and talked to him about Jesus and led him to the Lord."

"But he got hit by a bus! We all saw him."

The missionary brought the man over to our group so all the kids could see him. He had sustained some minor scrapes on his knees, and he was sore, but he was basically uninjured. More importantly, he was radiant, thanks to his new relationship with God.

Our kids were ecstatic that night when they saw the man who had been hit by our bus. He was alive and well and a supernatural miracle that they were able to witness firsthand. He was now a believer in Jesus, and that was even more amazing. The kids and adults returned home to Connecticut ready to tell the world about a God who is real.

Shannon and I stayed in Trumbull for sixteen years—so long, in fact, that some of the original seven kids we served in the youth group grew up and became leaders who had kids of their own in our youth group. Shannon and I felt happy and content, knowing that we were doing something significant and that our lives were having a positive impact on so many kids. We were a team. Our marriage was solid, and we were in love. Our dreams were coming true.

We had no clue that our dreams were about to turn into nightmares.

CHAPTER 13

A "FAMILY" AT LAST

As part of the pastoral staff of New Life Assemblies of God church, I went to a two-day district pastors' conference at a majestic, eighteenth-century cathedral. It had been purchased by the Liberty Assemblies of God in Shrewsbury, Massachusetts, a suburb of Worcester. The front of the building looked similar to Notre Dame Cathedral in Paris. The sanctuary seated about six hundred people and boasted spectacular woodwork throughout, hand-tooled by Norwegian shipbuilders. There I received a spiritual message from God that dramatically changed my life.

I had traveled to the conference along with our church's children's pastor, Andrew. When we arrived, we slipped into the sanctuary and took seats behind the pastors already assembled there. As part of the introduction to the conference, the hosts played a video featuring the new pastor of the church, Will Bard, who described some phenomenal spiritual events their congregation had recently experienced. Pastor Bard was a young, skinny-looking fellow who had come to the church only a few years earlier.

As I listened to Will Bard telling stories about what God was doing in and through their church, I suddenly heard a voice speaking to me.

I have rarely been the kind of person who says, "God told me" to do this or that. Ordinarily, I studied the Scripture, believed, prayed, and listened for God's voice. Usually, His direction came to me in my heart and mind as I trusted Him to guide me one step at a time or as I stepped out in faith and obedience to what I sensed He wanted me to do.

This was different.

To this day, I can't fully describe it, but I clearly heard what I felt sure was an audible voice saying, "You need to be here."

Liberty Church in Shrewsbury wasn't really looking for a pastor, as far as I knew. Nor was I planning to leave the Bridgeport area. Quite the contrary, I had assumed that I'd probably spend my life working at New Life and possibly retire there. Mark Evans, New Life's perceptive associate pastor, had even asked me, "What do you want to do in the future? I know you don't want to be a youth pastor forever."

Without hesitation I had told him, "I want your job. I want to be an administrator who can run the church. I don't need to be out front; I'm happy working behind the scenes, but I want to do something significant."

So I had not gone to the pastors' conference in Massachusetts trolling for new career opportunities. Moreover, the leaders in Worcester didn't know me, and I didn't know them. That's what was so weird about the message I sensed God speaking to me. There was no earthly, logical reason for it.

Later that day, I called Shannon, tried to explain what had happened, and said, "Babe, I need you to pray with me about this."

Shannon replied, "Jim, in all the years I've known you, there have been only a few times when you said that God told you to do something. I don't need to pray. Just do whatever He is asking you to do."

"Okay, but please pray!"

I didn't tell anyone else about the revelation I had received, but I pondered it overnight and through the conference the following day. I called my buddy, Tim Moen, another pastor friend who was attending the conference, and told him what I had experienced. "Tim, tell me about this church," I said. "Are they looking for someone on their pastoral staff?"

"I don't know," Tim said, "but I'm supposed to meet with Will Bard tomorrow. I'll let you know what I find out."

When Tim called me back, he was less than encouraging. "No, they aren't searching for anyone to hire right now," he said. "They need somebody, but they aren't ready yet, so I'm not sure what's going on."

I still felt strongly that I needed to consider the possibilities, so I said to Tim, "I'd love to talk with Pastor Will and tell him what happened to me."

"They're not looking for anyone," Tim reiterated, "but Will said that he'd be happy to hear what you had to say."

I talked to Will Bard by telephone about a week later and told him about the voice I had heard. "Man, I just feel that God is making some changes in my heart. The experience I had at the conference really stirred me."

Will listened graciously, then said, "I'm not sure why we'd offer you a job when you already have a job."

"I understand," I said. "But I am going to submit my resignation at New Life." I had already discussed the matter with Shannon before the phone call with Will, and she had agreed. We felt that, for some reason, our time at New Life was done.

Will and I agreed to keep talking and stay open to the possibilities.

A few days later, I went to Pastor Don and Pastor Mark, who I considered as family. "Hey, guys, this is going to be a weird conversation, but I feel like my time here is done."

"What?" Pastor Don said. "We don't want you to leave."

"Where are you going?" Pastor Mark asked, immediately assuming that I wouldn't leave unless I had an offer to go to a better job.

Suddenly, I became nervous. I had seen how some people in our congregation had responded when other members of our team had left our camp, and it was not a pretty sight. Maybe that's why I allowed fear to keep me from telling our pastors the whole truth about why I was leaving right away, but it probably wouldn't have mattered.

I fudged on the truth. I didn't really lie; I simply told a portion of what I knew in my heart, that somehow, some way, someday, I'd be moving to Massachusetts.

To the question about where I was going, I answered, "I don't know."

In fact, I really didn't know. The church in Massachusetts was not searching for an additional pastor, and I had no invitation from them even to apply for a position.

But I understood what my leaders were asking. And I didn't want to muddy the waters by having them offer me another position or more money or attempt to talk me out of leaving.

Pastor Don adamantly disagreed with my decision to leave. "God would not call you away without revealing the matter to us, the spiritual leaders to whom you are accountable. Nor would He call you to another congregation without speaking to the pastor there."

It was an uncomfortable feeling for me. I regarded Pastor Don as a spiritual father and felt as though Shannon and I were part of the Evans family. No wonder we were all conflicted. After all, I was telling them that I was leaving, but I couldn't tell them where I planned to go.

Almost every day after that meeting, my spiritual leaders nudged me for more information. "What's going on? Where are you going?"

Sometime that summer, I gave in and said, "Here's the bottom line: the reason I am not telling you where I'm going is that I believe God is leading me to Shrewsbury, Massachusetts. But they're not looking for anyone, and they haven't made any offers. So I don't know how God will direct me."

Pastor Don continued to disagree during our discussions of my plans. His son Mark was more open, at least ostensibly. "Well, Jimmy, we don't want to see you go," Mark said, "but let's trust God for how we should proceed. I wish you would have told us earlier. We need to talk about an exit strategy."

"Okay," I said tenuously. "What are you thinking?"

"Well, first of all, let's not tell anybody that you are leaving just yet," Mark advised. "Don't even tell your youth staff. After all, you've been here sixteen years, so we don't want to upset our people. And we don't have a replacement to offer them yet. So let's think in terms of making a public announcement this fall sometime. We'll have a big celebration, a going away party for you and Shannon, so we can bless you as we send you off to your new ministry."

"Okay, great!" I said.

It all sounded quite nice. It probably would have been fantastic had it worked out that way. But it didn't.

Somehow, the church leaders and I communicated our intentions inadequately, or perhaps we perceived matters differently. But it turned into an unnecessary mess.

I was conducting teen camp in July when I received a phone call from Jessica, one of my staff members. "Why didn't you tell me?" she wanted to know.

"Jessica, what are you talking about?"

"Well, I just heard that you have resigned and that you and Shannon will be moving on later this month."

I was stunned. Apparently, information had gotten out about my ensuing resignation without my knowledge.

"I'm sorry about that, Jessica. I don't know what is going on right now. Can I call you back?"

I immediately called our senior pastor, Pastor Don. When he answered, I said, "Hey, Boss, I just got a call from Jessica, and she was upset because she had heard that I have resigned. I'm a bit confused because you and Mark and I agreed that we will make a joint announcement and tell everyone together. I hate that my staff is finding this out at the same time as everyone else with no advance notice from me."

Pastor Evans let me rant for a moment or two longer, then he bluntly said, "James, I am the leader of this congregation and I decide what happens here."

I understood Pastor Don's words all too well. He was in charge. He was in control, not me, not even of my own resignation or future departure date.

"Okay," I said flatly. I didn't know what else I could answer. Pastor Don was my "spiritual leader," but he was also my boss. Besides, there was little I could do. I was leading a youth camp with more than four hundred teenagers. So I simply went back to work.

When I returned home after the camp, Pastor Don, Mark, and Jason all gathered to meet with me. "We just felt that stringing things along was not helpful," Mark explained. "We needed to move on it, so we made a decision. And you have told people that you are leaving, haven't you?"

"Yes, a few close friends," I answered.

"So the information that you are resigning has already gotten out."

"Well, not exactly. I just bounced some things off my closest friends."

"Nevertheless, we felt it best to move up our timetable," the pastor said, abruptly ending the conversation.

That's the way we left it for a few weeks, until at the close of a Sunday evening service, the pastors made an announcement regarding my resignation and departure. "We have some coffee and doughnuts in the fellowship hall, the side room over here, for those of you who would like to say goodbye to Pastor Jim and Shannon."

Caught totally off guard and unprepared to present a meaningful word of appreciation or any sort of departure speech, I simply gulped hard and smiled.

We had other expectations, but that was the "celebration," the blessing, and the send-off we received after serving the church for sixteen years.

PART IV

BAD THINGS HAPPEN

CHAPTER 14

BETRAYAL

When Shannon and I drove away from New Life Church following our send-off, we felt lost. Feelings of abandonment similar to those I had experienced during my childhood came flooding back to me and nearly overwhelmed me. As I had learned through my psychological studies, *perception matters*. Each of us has our own view of events; yet what we see isn't always accurate. We can't separate what we think from our perceptions of what we see, so our perspective matters enormously. Apparently, our perception of how we hoped to depart Trumbull was different from the church leadership's. I felt hurt and almost insulted, but I realized that was only my perception of what had happened. Most other people in the congregation probably had no clue about how our leaving had affected me.

We put our house up for sale and it sold within four days! That was a great encouragement to us as we began our transition. We left Trumbull and traveled to Virginia, where we moved in temporarily with my stepmom and my dad. We lived with them for seven months. I was no longer drawing a salary from my previous employer, so to pay our bills I worked on some construction projects with my dad. Shannon worked from home for a real estate office to help.

If there was a silver lining to our ignominious departure from the church in Connecticut, it was that our move to Virginia allowed me to develop a stronger relationship with my brother, Marcus. We spent time together, learning to scuba dive, and for the first time since our childhood, we had fun together. Marcus was aware of what had happened to us at New Life. I avoided talking with him about the details, and I was meticulous about making sure that I kept my conversation and comments about the church on the positive side.

Marcus noticed.

He knew that Shannon and I were still reeling as a result of our hasty departure from New Life and had every right to be bitter. He said to me one day, "Look, if there was a person I'd admire as a Christian, it's you, and if you have ever modeled true Christianity," he said to me, "you are demonstrating that right now."

To me, to hear that sort of backhanded compliment from my brother almost made my jacked-up resignation procedure worthwhile.

A friend of mine, Dick Hardy, worked as a Christian "headhunter," helping pastors and churches connect. Dick was confident he could help me find a new ministerial position. "There's a great church of about eight thousand people in the state of Indiana," he told me. "They are looking for a senior pastor and are interested in you. Jim, you'd be a great fit."

"But Dick, I don't want to be a senior pastor," I told him. "I don't need to be in the spotlight. I'm happy to work behind the scenes."

"Okay, Jim," he said. "I think it is crazy what you are doing, when we have these opportunities for you, but I guess you have to be true to the Lord and how He is guiding you."

"Thanks, Dick. That's what I'm trying to do," I said.

For more than five months I heard nothing from Will Bard and the church in Massachusetts.

During that time, however, I did receive two emails from Micah and Charlotte, the closest friends we had at New Life whom we had spent a great deal of time with and shared some of our deepest thoughts. Both emails contained overt invitations to return to the church. "Please come back," the emails urged. "We miss you and our children miss you."

Pastor Mark Evans had even written an email to me, suggesting that I would be the ideal candidate to start a new "southern-style church" north of New Life near Yale University. "You wouldn't have to do Sunday nights or Tuesday night services, and you wouldn't even have to wear a tie," Mark quipped. For many New England pastors, a tie, or even a ministerial robe, was the standard for the pulpit and leadership.

For some reason, I felt compelled to keep those emails I received, if for no other reason than they validated my worth in some way. After all, why would they want me to return if I had not done a good job? I knew that I had served well with all my heart, and these emails confirmed it.

Not long after that, I heard from Will Bard. "Jim, we are looking at two men, you and another guy." Will told me that the other person had earned a doctorate and had written books, but the congregation and staff liked me. "We like your style of preaching," he said, "and your leadership skills."

Then Will dropped a bomb. "But we do have an issue. A while ago, some people from your former church drove four hours to have a meeting with our leaders. They said that your résumé is fake."

"What?" I was flabbergasted by Will's statement. "Who would do such a thing?"

"Do the names Micah and Charlotte ring a bell?" Will asked.

"Of course," I said without hesitation. "They were some of Shannon's and my dearest friends at the church there. We were like family together. *They* said these things?"

"Yes," Will continued, "they said that everything on your résumé is a lie. Everything you said that you did while on staff there, you didn't really do."

"But anyone in our church could confirm what I did at New Life," I suggested.

"Yes, of course," Will agreed. "We know that. But your friends told us that you did not have a 'teachable spirit,' that the leadership there couldn't train you to be a good pastor, that you weren't really a good preacher. But Jim, we are not swayed by those statements. After all, the leaders kept you on the church staff in Trumbull for sixteen years and gave you increasing authority. The district office and the national office are well aware of your accomplishments.

"But," Will said, "the part we can't get past is what they said about you and the teenage girls. . . ."

"What!" I interrupted him. "What are you talking about, Will? What girls?"

Will seemed almost embarrassed that he had broached the subject. His voice was a gentle whisper as he said, "And they said that you had all these young girls as disciples coming to your house . . . and they were quick to include, 'We're not saying that anything happened, but it just didn't look right.'"

I couldn't believe my ears. There *were* young girls who came to our home in Connecticut all the time. Shannon and I hosted our youth leadership team of about eighteen kids, male and female, at our house every Friday night for years. We had transformed our basement into an arcade, so kids were at our house frequently. But nothing inappropriate ever happened at our home with any of those teens.

"The search committee is concerned about that. Would you like to answer these accusations?" Will said.

It was weird.

I tried hard to review and wrap my mind around these developments. Apparently a couple with whom Shannon and I had been close—some of the best examples of a Christian family that I had ever known—had traveled four hours out of their way to smear my reputation. They had made it sound as though my integrity was questionable and that I was missing something important, some indispensable ingredient necessary for ministry. Worse yet, they seemed to have implied that we had done something inappropriate involving the young guys and girls who often hung out at our home.

"Will, I don't know what to tell you except what you already know—that those things aren't true. But I'll tell you what I'll do. I have two recent emails from those same close friends at New Life. I will forward them to you and I'd appreciate it if you would read them with your search committee. Once you've read them, I have two options for you to consider. One, you can let me know, 'We have read the emails, and we're going to go with the other guy.' Or, 'Jim, we've read the emails, and we'd like to talk further with you.'

"I have only one caveat, Will," I continued. "If you choose option two, you all should know that I am not going to discuss these issues with the church leaders ever again. This matter is over and done. I don't want to serve under a cloud of suspicion. I didn't do anything wrong, so I'm not going to act as though I did." I sent Will the emails, convinced that God could defend my honor.

When I hung up the phone and told Shannon about the distortions and innuendos, she went on a warpath. She wanted to return to Connecticut and expose what "our friends" had done. While I was surprised and appreciative of her expressions of support, I attempted to calm her down. "No, Shannon, we don't have to defend ourselves. Don't let bitterness creep in. Don't allow who they are to change you."

Certainly, the couple's actions saddened and angered me, but I was not about to get into a skunk fight with anybody.

Will called back about an hour later. "I am so very sorry about the confusion," he said. "When can you come up to meet with us?"

"How about this weekend?" I suggested.

"Perfect."

I flew to Massachusetts that Saturday, met with the search committee and other leaders in the congregation, and they hired me as their executive pastor.

· · · · ·

With the money we pocketed from the sale of our home in Trumbull, Shannon and I decided to build our dream home in Massachusetts. Shannon stayed in Virginia for the first eight months that I was in Shrewsbury. I lived in a bed and breakfast while we waited for the construction of our beautiful new colonial-style home to be completed. I worked on church matters from early in the morning till late at night six days a week and flew home to Virginia whenever I could.

Liberty Assemblies of God church also hired Dr. George Claudis, the other candidate they had been considering. George and I had complementary skill sets. George brought expertise in financial matters, so he handled those aspects of the church, and I focused on the people's practical spiritual needs and how we could best meet them.

For all the appearances of spiritual vitality, the church in Shrewsbury was in a much more precarious position than I at first realized. But it didn't take long after arriving to discover that many parts of the ministry there were teetering and nearly ready to topple. Part of that started at the top.

Pastor Will and his wife's relationship was in trouble, and although many people in the congregation were unaware of it, the strain in his marriage affected everything Will did. Although a visionary with a gentle spirit and tremendous faith, Will was desperately lacking in administration skills. Consequently, with Will distracted, there had been nobody to pick up the slack, and the church staff was highly dysfunctional. They hadn't even had a real staff meeting in more than a year before I came on board. They had scores of active ministries because anytime someone approached the pastoral leaders and suggested a new idea, they'd say, "Go ahead." Many of those ministries overlapped or duplicated work that was already being done.

When the church hired me, I promised them, "I'll change that for you." I immediately set about streamlining and organizing the ministries of the church. I encouraged the staff to ask questions such as "So what? Why does this matter? Now what? What are we going to do? What's the next step?" This practical approach worked. We continued to grow exponentially, drawing crowds of more than three thousand people on Sundays. We held multiple services each week with more than fifty people on our staff. We built teams, taught leadership principles, and allowed people to take responsibility.

We soon initiated another building program as well as a Dream Center, a ministry to drug and alcohol abusers. On a separate campus, the church operated a daycare center and also provided space for ancillary ministries. The congregation loved people, and we reached out compassionately to our community. At Christmastime, church members scoured the malls and toy stores, searching for just the right toys and purchasing gifts for thousands of children. A lot of good things were happening in, around, and through the church.

For the first few years I was there, the church was booming. People were coming from everywhere, and the ministry was thriving. Unfortunately, two major incidents occurred that set us on our heels. First, Pastor Will stepped back from actively leading the ministry, feeling that he needed to take a break, even though he wanted to remain involved. But other than preaching, he rarely showed up at the church. More and more, I stepped into a primary leadership role with the staff and the congregation.

The second incident was that I met a woman named Vanessa.

CHAPTER 15

When the Golden Rule Doesn't Work

Shannon and I felt that we were solid in our marriage relationship. She was quiet, demure, incredibly sweet, and committed to keeping the peace in our home. And I was . . . well, *me*! Gregarious, loud, and so adept at presenting a confident image, I worked hard at coming off as the quintessential answer man. Not surprisingly, some people assumed I was arrogant, or at best, cocky. In my better moments, I admitted that I could be a pompous prig.

Despite our differences, Shannon and I genuinely loved each other. In fact, we were so wonderfully convinced that we were good together, we both felt we were God's special gift to each other. Sure, we had typical spats, similar to most couples, but nothing out of the ordinary. If someone had asked us, "Do you think you are in a bad marriage?" we would have been appalled and answered emphatically, "Certainly not!" But we were disconnected when it came to intimacy—not necessarily sexual intimacy, but emotional intimacy—and we didn't even know it.

Since then, I've met many people who have felt similarly. Many couples sense that their marriage is in trouble or possibly even over, but they can't figure out why, so they have lost hope that anything can change for the better, apart from divorce. That creates a cosmic-sized loneliness in a person's heart, even if that person is surrounded by people. I've heard many a man or woman say, "I thought I was the only person who ever felt this way." And that is how I felt, lost in an inexplainable loneliness, even while being in close proximity to my wife every day.

Looking back, it's easy to see that I was running hard and heading for a cliff, but at the time, I had no comprehension that I felt invisible and insecure, unappreciated, and, in some sense, abandoned. But I did. I simply had not articulated those feelings to Shannon, and in truth, maybe I had never genuinely admitted those emotions to myself. Part of the problem was the negative view I held of myself.

Even when I did something good or accomplished some special goal, my mindset that I had developed over the years was to denigrate myself and say things such as, "Well, it's not really me. It's God. It's Jesus." All of which were true. It *was* God working in and through *me*. But He hadn't turned me into a robot. I was still involved in what He was doing. In fact, making myself available to Him made all the difference in my life.

Ironically, my supposed piety and my unwillingness to take credit for any good deeds I had done produced in me a passively aggressive attitude, even toward God!

I was starving for affirmation and often became resentful when someone else received accolades. Meanwhile I was stewing in my spiritual mush, quoting John the Baptist's words about Jesus: "He must increase; I must decrease."

Simultaneously, I felt cheated. *Look at all I am doing*, I thought. *Why haven't they said anything nice about me?* Even when someone tried to compliment me, I couldn't receive it. So I was trapped in a chimerical dance—I longed to be wrapped in the arms of affirmation and appreciation, yet when it brushed even close to me, I pushed off, twirled away, and backpedaled. I was alone again.

I had yet to learn that there is a cooperative work that God does in and through us that gives Him the glory but allows us to participate in His plans. For all my biblical knowledge, that truth somehow eluded me or, at best, never settled in my heart and mind.

In that sense, the Golden Rule as put forth by Jesus (do unto others as you'd have them do unto you) simply didn't work for Shannon and me. Why? Because Shannon and I placed different values on what love meant to us. We knew we loved each other, but our "love languages" were radically different. My love languages are words of affirmation and touch, but those were ineffective when I assumed that Shannon wanted the same. Her love languages, means of expression, and expectations were much different from mine. She much preferred acts of service and spending quality time together, so if I kept the house tidy or came home from work early for no other reason but to be with her, she regarded that as a marvelous expression of love—even if we did nothing more than watch a movie together. Consequently, she assumed those things would mean something special to me. But they didn't.

Shannon often bought and gave me beautiful cards expressing her love for me. I appreciated the gesture, but greeting cards did not evoke much of a response from me. I read them, thanked her, and threw them away. That offended Shannon. So treating each other the way we individually wanted to be treated failed to elicit positive results. Although it would be a number of years before we learned it, unless our loving expressions communicated that we loved, liked, and respected each other, they were doomed to fail.

My emotional deficiencies permeated our marriage, although neither of us would have consciously been aware of those things or able to express them during the first twenty years of our relationship. Whenever anyone asked us about our marriage, we always declared our love for each other and gushed about what a great relationship we enjoyed.

We were telling the truth, too, as much as we knew of it, but there was trouble brewing in paradise. Here's why:

At that time, I lived and operated based on my personal perceptions—I stewed on how I felt whenever somebody said or did something that directly affected me, especially if that person was Shannon. My most vulnerable areas involved feeling abandoned or that I was insignificant and didn't matter. So if Shannon said or did something that touched any of those nerves, I recoiled—even if she had no idea that she had said or done something to elicit a negative reaction in me.

"I'm going to the grocery store," Shannon said. "Do you need anything?"

"Oh, no, I'm fine," I replied. "Oh, wait, I'd really love to have some Necco wafers." Since childhood, I have always loved the rolls of candy wafers, each one tasting like the color—brown ones taste like chocolate, black ones taste like licorice, red ones taste like cherry; you get the idea. I knew that not every store sold them, but the grocery store where Shannon shopped most frequently usually carried a supply in their candy section.

"Okay, anything else?" Shannon asked.

"Well, if they are fresh, I'd really like some grapes too."

"Is that everything?"

"Yes, that's all."

An hour or two later, Shannon returned home toting several large bags of groceries in the car. I helped her unload the bags from the trunk to the kitchen, my eyes searching in each bag for my sweet delights.

We unloaded all the groceries, and still I saw no Necco wafers and no grapes. Shannon had purchased plenty of meat, bread, eggs, milk, coffee, and all sorts of other groceries, including personal items for herself. But no Necco wafers or grapes.

I didn't say anything about the omission, but I stewed over it for the rest of the day. She had gotten everything else we could possibly need, but she had forgotten my Necco wafers and grapes. And I was miffed about it.

Was I being silly? Childish? Selfish?

Maybe.

But while the missing Necco wafers and grapes may seem like such a minor deal to most people, Shannon's neglect spoke volumes to me. I've said it before: perception is reality for most of us. From my perspective, what I perceived was this: "Apparently what I wanted, what I enjoyed, did not matter to her." It was a small step to extrapolate that out to thinking, *I do not matter to her.* If she really cared for me, she would have made sure she purchased my candy treats and grapes. I must be unimportant, insignificant, and invisible to her. She must not respect me. She must not love me; she must not care.

No matter how many marvelous things Shannon said to me or did for me, those minor forgotten details took precedence. She did care for me deeply, but I didn't believe it any longer. Even her words, "I love you," lacked authentic meaning to me because of the doubts that loomed behind the missing Necco wafers and grapes.

Add up enough similar minor offenses, oversights, absences, late nights at work, or other emotion-laden infractions, and without consciously choosing to do so, we allowed intimacy to disappear. At the same time, we opened a door to marital infidelity.

Nevertheless, every morning, I got up and told Shannon, "I love you." It was a practice I maintained, and I meant those words sincerely. I felt that if I thought those thoughts and said the words, they would turn into actions. "See it, believe it, and achieve it" all stemmed from a volitional decision. I understood that oft-quoted adage: "Love is a choice." And it is! But love also implies actions. To me, for Shannon to merely say the words without backing them up by her actions—on issues both bigger and smaller than grapes and Neccos—produced more fodder for frustrations and fights. And although neither of us had a clue regarding our lack of emotional intimacy, those frustrations percolated just below the surface, like a seething volcano ready to explode and pour hot lava all over us, incinerating the bonds of our marriage.

I couldn't really blame Shannon for not perceiving my emotional needs. I never spoke of them to her at that time, and I am not certain why I got so put out over such little things. But they weren't little to me.

After all, if Shannon said to me, "Jim, would you please clean up your beard shavings on the bathroom sink," I would certainly make sure the sink was spotless. Why couldn't she do something similar for me without me having to harp on it? Didn't she realize what that did to me?

No, she didn't; she couldn't. She did not understand that I was so susceptible and vulnerable to her innocent omissions because I approached every human relationship already feeling deficient, insignificant, and invisible. So if she told me she was going to do something and didn't, I took it personally as an expression of her disrespect.

Shannon never really knew me as a person with fears and insecurities. To her, I was always the strong one. It wasn't fair on my part, but I assumed that Shannon would not respond well if I told her about my inadequacies. Even if I tried to explain my feelings, I didn't want to dump a heavy load on her. After all, I felt responsible for her. I knew from nearly two decades of our marriage that if I attempted to bring something to her attention regarding my innermost thoughts and feelings, asking her opinion or requesting her help, her usual response was, "I don't know" or "Whatever you think." After a while, I stopped trying to approach her about any of my deepest needs. Making matters worse, I could not articulate those needs well and may not even have been completely aware of them myself at the time.

I began building a wall in our relationship that I could not see. Shannon didn't see the real bricks stacked in the wall, since on her side of it, all she could see was what I wanted her to see, all the good things about our life together, which meant all the good things I felt she needed to see to accept me. I couldn't trust her to take care of other areas, so I made decisions for Shannon, I kept her safe, I was her protector, provider, and spiritual adviser.

More significantly, in times when I did attempt to confess a fear or failure to Shannon and she rejected or attacked me for it or responded with what seemed to me as indifference, I put up more bricks. I made it hard for us to experience intimacy. Behind my brick wall, I felt safe, and on the other side of it, Shannon seemed oblivious to anything that might be souring in our marriage. How could she do otherwise? On her side of the wall, I had painted a picture of the "me" that I felt she needed to see so she would accept me.

For my part, even though we had an active sex life together, I did not feel intimacy or passion, only commitment. I should have recognized that commitment alone was not enough to keep our marriage healthy. But I didn't. Ironically, I was a pastor and a counselor to others. Yet I failed to see the deficiencies in my own life.

CHAPTER 16

ADDICTED TO "LOVE"

N or did I see any danger when I met Vanessa, a younger, married woman on our church worship team—the musical ensemble that led the congregation in singing each week and helped facilitate others to enter into God's presence. The music at the church was phenomenal.

We had numerous professional, studio-quality musicians serving with us, and the leader was a graduate of a prestigious music school. Melissa Gonzales, who had formerly sung with Carol Cymbala and the Brooklyn Tabernacle Choir, was also on the team.

As the pastor, especially one who enjoyed singing, I worked closely with the worship team to "map out" our services, deciding which songs, prayer times, celebration of communion, and other parts of the service would coordinate best with the message I planned to preach to the congregation each week.

The musicians and the singers wanted to keep our focus on God and not "quench the Spirit," so we tried to fit each service within certain time constraints and to lead the congregation in a somewhat predictable response. It wasn't manipulation; it was organization, something our church had been lacking for a while. We especially needed that sort of structure once our church began conducting a Saturday night service and three services each Sunday morning.

So the worship team and I met to plan and practice together every Thursday, sometimes several times in a week if we were doing a special presentation. I always looked forward to being with the musicians and singers, and I especially looked forward to seeing Vanessa, one of the main singers in the group.

Vanessa was a friend of ours, even though she was nineteen years younger than me. She was an attractive blonde, although certainly no more beautiful than my wife. She possessed a "cuteness" about her, but she didn't catch my attention because of her physical beauty or her intellectual, emotional, or spiritual attributes. Nor did she give off an overt sexuality that I picked up on. I did notice, however, her vivacious, bubbly personality and spirit.

She was witty in our conversations, with a bit of the sardonic, smart-aleck attitude similar to my own. We bounced wisecracks off each other with amazing humor—humor that others on the team often did not even catch. Many of our mutual friends just shrugged their shoulders at Vanessa's or my sardonic comments. Shannon was always quick to laugh at my jokes and had a good sense of humor, too, but hers was more linear: A plus B equals laughter. Vanessa possessed a fun, offbeat humor that kept me on my toes intellectually, looking for ways I could match her or, better yet, top her. I felt comfortable with my whimsical, flirtatious comments to Vanessa because, at that time, I was convinced that the greatest temptation to infidelity was sexual attraction. That, with God's help, I could control.

Most of all, Vanessa made me feel good about *me*. Not surprisingly, I hit it off with her better than anyone else on the worship team, and before long, we established an emotional connection.

Vanessa and her husband, Keith, were a fun couple and became close friends with Shannon and me. Keith was not on the worship team but helped with the sign language ministry. The four of us were constantly together at church, and we often went out to eat together after services. We even went on vacation together to "Bike Week," a huge motorcycle and music festival in Massachusetts. We occasionally went line dancing together with some other couples from the church, and Vanessa and Keith often came over to our house for dinner and to watch movies together.

At one point, when Vanessa learned that Shannon and I were still hoping to have a child and exploring every option, including the possibility of recruiting a surrogate mother, she ecstatically gushed to Shannon, "I would love to be your surrogate and carry your baby!" Her gracious offer didn't strike us as odd since we were such good friends, and there was nothing inappropriate about our relationship at that time.

Because we had new insurance coverage, we were able to have another in vitro procedure in Massachusetts. After the fertilized egg had been implanted in Shannon, she was lying in the hospital bed, groggy from the medications, and with the surgery cap still on her head, but she looked absolutely radiant. "I'm so happy right now," Shannon said as she looked over at me. Sadly, our happiness would be short-lived, as that in vitro procedure, too, proved unsuccessful.

Shannon finally gave up on the idea of having a baby. "Fine," she quipped, only half-joking. "If I can't have a baby, I want a convertible." I knew she was speaking out of her grief. Nevertheless, later that summer, I went out and purchased a brand new, green MINI-Cooper with tan and black leather interior for her, complete with a black convertible top.

• • • • •

Increasingly, I sought out my "buddy" Vanessa for many activities, especially anytime I wanted to have fun. "Where's Vanessa?" I'd ask Keith or Shannon, because I knew we'd have more fun together if she were involved. I wasn't trying to "hit on" her; I simply felt better when she was around. By her actions and attitudes, I felt respected and important.

As we grew closer and spent more time together as friends, she seemed more comfortable about sharing personal details with me regarding her relationship with Keith. I didn't offer any answers, but I commiserated with her. After a while, I did the same with her, talking about some of my frustrations cautiously at first, then more openly. I realized that she accepted me as I was: she heard me when I spoke, and she wanted to please me.

For instance, one day at church, Vanessa and I noticed that a mutual female friend had changed the color of her hair. "Wow, doesn't she look fabulous as a brunette?" I casually commented.

"I agree with you," Vanessa replied.

Two days later, when Vanessa came to the church, she was a brunette. I didn't ask whether it was an experiment or whether she wanted to please me, perhaps thinking that I found brunettes more attractive than blondes. I didn't say a word about her change in hair color. But I certainly noticed.

I'm an affectionate and emotional person by nature, so it felt natural to hug friends—male and female—who were close to me. Most of my family members are the same way, expressive Louisiana French Cajun people. So hugging Vanessa did not seem inappropriate or unusual to me or to Shannon. I wasn't looking for anything untoward or intending to communicate anything more through our hugs than simple expressions of affection. Our hugs were totally innocuous and often took place in front of Shannon and Keith and members of the church worship team without anyone raising an eyebrow. More and more, however, I noticed that Vanessa and I hugged a few seconds longer than necessary.

Unwittingly, we both were lowering our walls and finding acceptance in each other, and that built intimacy and caring feelings. I often said words such as, "I love you, come here, I want to hug you. You look great." Those were the same words I might say to someone else, but when I said them to Vanessa, the words began to take on deeper meanings. Slowly but surely, we were falling in love with each other.

Before long, I began burning up her cell phone, calling her for any reason, or no apparent reason, certainly nothing that related to the worship team or group activities with her, Keith, and Shannon. We exchanged voluminous text messages, often sending funny remarks to each other throughout the day, always bringing a smile to my face.

I realized, *This isn't right.* Yet I kept stepping across the line between appropriate and inappropriate.

Emotion trumps logic every time. Emotion can even trump spirit (and may even cause us to ignore the Spirit) if we allow it to do so. And I chose to allow it. I knew that I was living in a manner inconsistent with my values, what I believed to be true. I had firm beliefs about what is right and wrong. So something within me said, *What I am doing right now is wrong, even though I am not actually committing adultery.* I knew that, based on my beliefs and values, I was crossing lines and shouldn't be so close to Vanessa or any female other than Shannon. Yet I allowed it to continue.

But that created an even bigger problem for me: Did I really believe what I had always said I believed? Or were my feelings for Vanessa more important to me, even more important than my feelings for God or Shannon?

I convinced myself that my basic Christian beliefs had not changed, yet I compartmentalized them, keeping them separate from my actions and emotions. *As long as the three don't touch, I'm okay*, I assumed.

Silly me. I couldn't have been more wrong.

Vanessa, Keith, Shannon, and I were in group settings most of the time, but in any group, there were always people with whom I was more comfortable being around than others. Vanessa was the person with whom I felt most comfortable interacting, even in a group environment with a number of other couples. We didn't stick out a great deal at first, but simply because we talked together more frequently, laughed together, and acted differently around each other, people noticed. A few friends raised their eyebrows or nudged one another when they saw Vanessa and me laughing or carrying on. But nobody said anything. No one challenged us or said, "You two need to be careful. You are putting out a message you may not intend to communicate." Not even Shannon or Keith confronted Vanessa or me about our playful behavior.

I noticed a subtle change in my own attitude when I received another text message from Vanessa and quickly felt that I needed to delete it. *Wait a minute*, I thought. *Why do I feel compelled to delete a message from a friend?*

Hmm, maybe because there were dozens of text messages preceding that one. We were communicating by text message more than Shannon and I were or ever had!

Or perhaps Vanessa had moved out of the friend category, or maybe both of us had, and we now considered each other "more than friends."

I found myself thinking of Vanessa more than fifty percent of my waking hours, and that percentage seemed to be rising rather than diminishing. We continued texting back and forth every day. Often, we joked with each other, and occasionally, I noticed that a joke went too far, so we'd attempt to backpedal a bit. "If someone saw this," I wrote to her, "they would think wrongly of us. So let's just hide that. Make sure you clear your phone and delete messages. Because if Keith read that, it could sound bad."

"Oh, yeah, you're right," Vanessa texted back.

We were setting ourselves up for failure and too blinded by our feelings to see it. The lines between right and wrong—that had once been so clearly delineated—were increasingly becoming more blurred, at least to us.

I'm not going to have sex with this woman, I rationalized, *but our playful banter is fun and feels so good!*

The emotions of forbidden love are powerfully compelling, so much so that a person may be willing to go against everything he or she knows or believes. "How can it be wrong when it feels so right?" hundreds of songs, books, and movies have asked. Most people who have gotten caught up in affairs ask that same thing. They know they should walk away, but they don't.

Many Christians pretend that the Spirit of God will put them on autopilot and that He will supernaturally veer them away from temptation. I doubt it.

In truth, I didn't buy that thinking at all. From what I had learned of Scripture, I understood that with every temptation, God will make a way of escape, but I still had to walk through that way. I needed to ask God to show me the way He had provided so I could escape a particular temptation. Then I had to willfully take that path. I believed that God would help me to do that, but the responsibility to walk through that way of escape was mine.

No doubt, there were plenty of times when Vanessa and I almost got busted, and I felt as though God were saying to me, "Dude, I'm giving you chances right now. I'm providing opportunities for you to escape that temptation. You need to walk through those doors. I won't kick you through the doors or drag you away from temptation. The next move is yours."

I realized that the way of escape might not be painless. I had seen evidence of that in the lives of dozens of couples with whom I had counseled over the years. Choosing to embrace and act on temptation always has consequences. Often, those consequences are long-lasting and affect other people we love. Choosing to walk away from temptation can be equally tough and tumultuous, sometimes involving ridicule, embarrassment, emotional pain, and often spiritual disillusionment.

In my ministry over the years, I'd actually warned numerous other men and women about these truths. "If you have sex with someone to whom you are not married, or get involved in a sexual affair, the ramifications of your actions, even after you have sought the forgiveness of God, each other, and anyone else who was involved, will be with you for the rest of your life."

Knowing all that, I still continued to cross lines with Vanessa— because it felt so good. We became almost like drug addicts, craving each other constantly.

CHAPTER 17

SUSPICIONS

Shannon trusted me totally, and at first she had no suspicions about Vanessa, although my wife later said, "I started to see things that struck me as not quite right."

I ordinarily tried to be attentive and considerate of Shannon. "Can I get you anything? Can I do something for you? Can I fix your plate?"

But Shannon noticed that I was doing something similar for a woman to whom I was not married. I didn't even recognize that I had fallen into that habit, but Shannon did. She later said that she wondered, *Why is he doing those things for Vanessa?*

Shannon was not necessarily the jealous type, and with our sort of work, it was necessary to interact with women and girls frequently, so she was accustomed to seeing me talking with another woman or even hugging a woman from our congregation or someone from our group of friends. But occasionally, she would caution me about Vanessa. "I think you're getting a little close."

"Oh, don't be silly," I replied. "We're good friends. I'm allowed to have female friends, right?"

Shannon bit her lip, raised her eyebrows, and said, "Hmm, I don't know. I don't think you should be best friends with this girl."

We both knew that Vanessa was more outgoing than Shannon and her personality worked well with the members of the worship team and with mine. But there was still no indication to me that something was "too close."

I was gone from home for long hours almost every day, and even when I was at home with Shannon, Vanessa was with us a lot. Just friends. She often rode home after church with me in my pickup truck, and Keith frequently joined us later at Shannon's and my home.

The stress in my life was getting to me, and on one occasion, when Keith and Vanessa were staying overnight in the guest room at our house, I actually passed out in the shower. When I came to, they helped me up and wanted to take me to the hospital. "You go get the car," Vanessa said to Shannon, "and I will help Jimmy down the stairs."

Shannon dutifully retrieved our car while Keith and Vanessa helped me down the stairs, her arms tightly wrapped around me. She assisted me in getting into the car, and Shannon drove us to the hospital.

I had recently begun taking over-the-counter vitamins, so in the hospital, Vanessa whispered to Shannon, "Tell the doctor about his vitamins."

How did Vanessa know about those vitamins? I wondered. I bet Shannon wondered too. I must have told her, but I was reluctant to inform the doctor. When Shannon suggested that I tell the doctor about the vitamins, I rebuffed her, wanting to avoid further conversation about the vitamins and downplaying Vanessa's knowledge of my personal matters. Shannon might not have thought it odd that Vanessa knew about the vitamins since we were all so close and the four of us did so many things together. But more and more, Shannon picked up on other signals that Vanessa and I displayed.

One night, we all went line dancing, and Vanessa and I were lost in our own dance. Vanessa sat near me most of the evening. Shannon waited for an opportunity to speak to Vanessa alone and then confronted her. "You need to stay away from my husband," she said emphatically.

Vanessa stared back at Shannon as though offended.

"I'm watching you," Shannon said firmly.

Vanessa came to me and told me. I was furious. I walked over to Shannon and kissed her on the lips, then with a smirk, I said, "You've already lost me. Be quiet."

On another occasion, we were out together with two other people from church, and Vanessa and I were holding hands under the table. Shannon noticed. She cast an accusatory look at me and quietly said, "I saw that."

I leaned over and growled in her ear, "There are other people here. Be quiet."

Shannon remained quiet, but I knew she had caught me. When we returned home, Shannon tried to broach the subject, but I blew her off with a sarcastic, mean remark. "I don't value your opinion enough to even have that conversation," I snipped.

She continued to be still, knowing that if she made a commotion, I would retaliate or just walk out the door. Later I found out her attitude was, "Okay, God, I'm not going to say or do anything. I'm just going to be still and believe that You are in charge."

Although I didn't know it, she began reading books about men in a midlife crisis, how to be a better wife, and how to tell if your husband or wife is in an affair. The insights she gained from the books were helpful and encouraging to Shannon, but they really didn't touch the emotions I felt, especially my feelings of insignificance.

Keith and Vanessa accompanied Shannon and me to a festival called The Big E. As usual, Vanessa and I were playing off each other and were talking and laughing together. Shannon brushed by us and said, "You better be careful, Jimmy, people are going to start seeing things."

"Well, we're not doing anything," I huffed.

Shannon had been losing weight, most likely due to the stress on her nerves from worrying that something was going on. She had not mentioned her concerns to anyone in the church, especially to the church leaders, but had continued holding everything inside her. "Who could I go to?" she lamented years later. "Jimmy was the pastor! Who could I tell? I was alone in Massachusetts without any family members nearby. Most of my new friends were members of the church. How could I talk to someone about my husband's conduct?" Consequently, she didn't seek counsel or go to a support group. Nor did she nag me or treat me with disdain. She continued to love me the best ways she knew how.

When we went to a festival or some other event, I usually bought Shannon something to commemorate the event—a T-shirt, sweatshirt, belt, or some other article of clothing. "Oh, this would be cute for you," I'd say.

At the Big E festival, Vanessa and I spotted an attractive belt, and I pointed it out to Shannon. "Oh, that's really cute," she said. "Are you thinking of buying that for me?"

I turned on her. "You know, it's not all about you!" I snapped loudly. Other people jerked their heads, looking to see what was going on. I twirled around and said to Vanessa, "See, it's always about her, never about me."

Vanessa and I walked away and left Shannon standing there in shock. I knew she wouldn't call out. She knew that would hurt my reputation, so she simply stood there quietly. "God helped me to hold it together," Shannon would recall.

Later that day, we regrouped, and Keith, Shannon, Vanessa, and I walked over to the performance area where there was to be a country music show. The country shows were some of Shannon's favorites. We climbed the bleachers, and I sat down next to Shannon—with Vanessa on my other side, thigh to thigh, her leg pressed warmly against mine. Right where I wanted it to be.

To anyone else, it all appeared normal, just friends out together with friends, but Shannon seemed to sense that there was more going on. And there was.

CHAPTER 18

MOVING IN A DANGEROUS DIRECTION

During my second and third years at the Liberty church, I was counseling and preaching more, especially with Will still on the sidelines, but mostly, I was all about setting our vision, building our team, and moving forward.

In contrast, we had a member of our board of directors pushing to construct another building. He wanted to keep adding to our facility, an asset already worth more than $20 million, including more and more nice, but unnecessary, accoutrements. I appreciated his faith and enthusiasm, but I preferred that we keep our focus on building *people* rather than buildings. "Do we really need a waterfall in our baptistry?" I asked. "Or a granite-topped outdoor barbecue pit?" Personally, I didn't think we needed the opulence. We debated back and forth, and these discussions caused a great deal of tension internally. I tried to stay focused on the need. When you add more buildings, you add more of everything: programs, people, the works, so there was plenty to keep me busy.

In numerous meetings, I said to our leadership group, "Slow down, because once you get into that sort of expenditure and are committed to it, you have the added stress of the financial responsibilities." But we pushed forward nonetheless and began a major building project. We were conducting about four or five services each weekend. Then we added a Saturday night service as well. So the construction seemed necessary and was probably inevitable.

We were busy, working constantly, and were meeting our budgetary goals, so for a while, although it was stressful, we were brimming with confidence. Then the 2008 real estate market crashed, adding even more pressure to our stretched and strained budget. We had already begun the massive new building project, so we couldn't simply quit. Consequently, we needed to bring in $50,000 each week merely to pay expenses. Although we had grown our congregation to about three thousand people, we weren't close to reaching five thousand anytime soon, so there was little hope of relieving the financial pressure through sheer charitable giving. All we could do was cut spending where possible and plow forward.

As the senior pastor, Will stepped in occasionally and joined us in our discussions, but for the most part, he had checked out emotionally. He preached and showed up at staff meetings sporadically. For nearly a year, he allowed himself to be out of the flow of what was going on at the church. When he did show up, the rest of us on staff were elated to see him while at the same time almost amused at his attitude.

One staff member joked, "Here we go again—rainbows and unicorns." Everyone laughed nervously, but it really wasn't funny. Will had such tremendous faith that he operated on a mystical level, always naively believing for the best. "Oh, isn't everything marvelous? God is going to see us through, and it is going to be better in the days ahead than it ever was in the past."

We all wanted to say "Amen" to that, but all too often, reality poked holes in our balloons of idealism—most of which were launched by Will. Everything *wasn't* beautiful. We had major issues we needed to confront, but Will didn't have the emotional bandwidth for that. Like many great spiritual motivators, Will tended to "hypercontexualize" the Scripture, stretching the meaning to imply what he wanted it to say or mean. For example, in speaking about "God calling into being that which does not exist" from Romans 4, Will might express that God wants to do miracles in our lives, based on that Scripture. He didn't misquote it; he simply invested the words with meaning that the original author may not have intended. His attitude was "Let's just operate in faith, believing God."

Okay. But we still needed to pay the bills and make some changes.

Looking back, I can now understand that Will had so many other things going on in his life that it was hard for him to deal in specifics when it came to the church. Regardless, although I had signed on with him as an executive pastor, increasingly I shouldered more of the leadership responsibilities, as well as the speaking duties.

We were working through the difficulties associated with multiple services on multiple campuses and still attempting to maintain a consistent message. That was easy unless something unusual happened at one location that hadn't occurred at the other. For instance, if someone spoke out an unexpected "word of prophecy" at one of the churches, we attempted to inform the congregation on the other campuses so we could all be on the same spiritual page. More and more, our growth became more stressful for me.

I tried to share some of my concerns with Shannon, and she sympathized with me, but she had no suggestions. Nor did I expect any from her.

The one place I found solace and encouragement was in the presence of Vanessa.

• • • • •

Vanessa stepped off the platform after singing with the worship team. She sat down and looked at me as I began to preach the message. The affirmation and adoration that I saw in her eyes made my heart beat more rapidly. We both knew our attitudes and actions were moving in a dangerous direction, but somehow, we were able to set that truth aside while we served in our assigned roles. We knew that God's Word was true, whether we represented Him well or not, whether we were thinking and living according to His Word or not. Despite all that we knew or believed, we willfully chose to ignore His instructions.

Yet I was a preacher of the gospel. I had seen and heard enough preachers over the years to know that while most were genuine, some were total charlatans. I was also aware that in the Old Testament book of Numbers, God had used a jackass to speak truth and that Balaam, who was a warped, profit-minded prophet, still spoke truth in spite of himself, though his actions and their ramifications were later condemned in the Bible.

When I preached, I knew I was a hypocrite, but I preached with no less conviction. I recognized that I had a responsibility to present a helpful message because thousands of people were showing up each week looking for hope. I was the dealer of hope. I wasn't preaching *against* sin so much as preaching *for* a relationship with God. I believed that if people discovered a loving relationship with God, that would allow a refining process to work in their lives and help them avoid sin. It did in most people's hearts and minds, but not in mine.

When I walked off the platform, it was really hard for me to deal with the contradictions in my life. I knew I was doing wrong by letting my thoughts and feelings about Vanessa get out of control, and it wasn't that I didn't care. I cared deeply, but I rationalized that God understood my heart—and no doubt, He did. All too well. But that allowed me to live and function with the dichotomy between what I *believed* that I believed and what I knew to be true.

CHAPTER 19

CROSSING THE LINE

It was at least a year after I arrived at Liberty when I became totally enamored with Vanessa. We were often together in groups and sometimes even alone with each other. Anytime Vanessa touched my hand, my arm, or my shoulder, the mere sensation of her fingers on my skin sent emotional electricity surging throughout my entire body. But I didn't think her touches were out of line. We were both affectionate, "touchy-feely" type of people. We hugged each other frequently. But we moved into dangerous waters when Keith and Vanessa and Shannon and I went on a cruise together. As couples, we had shared previous vacations together and had handled the togetherness well, but something about having more downtime together aboard the ship allowed Vanessa and me to gravitate toward each other.

More and more, I viewed Vanessa with a sort of "halo effect," seeing only her good points while minimizing her flaws. It felt "intimate," but in fact, that intimacy was fatuous and unreal. True intimacy occurs only in safety, and adulterous affairs cannot provide that. Nevertheless, the halo effect allowed me to ignore Vanessa's flaws and focus only on the good feelings I experienced when I was with her. I felt compelled to move forward. Vanessa and I had been talking for a long time. We knew each other and liked each other. But when we lowered our walls and allowed intimacy to develop, as much as I tried to pretend that I could handle the temptations, I couldn't.

Vanessa had confided in me about some of her struggles in her marriage to Keith, so that opened my compassion valve, and I felt closer to her. So close, in fact, that she was the first person I ever let know that I had been sexually molested as a child. Sharing such intimate descriptions lowered our boundary walls even further and created a false sense of intimacy. She did not view me negatively because of my past experiences and seemed to accept me fully for who I was, warts and all. At that point, I felt more connected to her than to anyone else in my life—including Shannon.

One day, I was sitting on a rock outside our house and smoking a cigar, looking out over a field when it hit me: *I think I am in love with this woman!*

I walked back to the house and called Vanessa. "We can't do this," I said. "We're good people; we have good spouses. We need to fix this."

"Yes, I know," Vanessa agreed.

For a while, we stepped more carefully around our feelings, but at that point, we were emotionally connected and didn't want to stop.

We did not make overtly sexual statements to each other, such as, "I want to make love to you," or other blatant seductions. But Vanessa and I often spoke in code about the possibility of us taking a step toward having sexual intercourse with each other. We traded comments laced with subtle sexual innuendos. For instance, one of us might say, "You're crazy," with the other firing back, "You couldn't *handle* this crazy." We'd both laugh, but the comments piqued our imaginations and drew us increasingly closer to the line between friendly jesting and inappropriate seduction. We had already crossed that line in our hearts and minds, emotionally and spiritually, much earlier, long before we made it convenient to cross those lines physically.

Vanessa was often home during the day, so we made plans to meet at a neutral location where we both knew we would be alone. On the way, I stopped at a grocery store to purchase some condoms. I had been married for twenty years and had never bought condoms, so I was nervous as I hopped out of my truck and went inside the store, searching the aisles. I made the purchase and hurried back to my pickup and started pulling away. Just then, I saw a guy from our church pulling into the grocery store parking lot. I literally ducked my head down below the dashboard so he wouldn't see me. *What am I doing?* I thought. *Who cares if someone sees me at the grocery store?* My nerves were frazzled, and I could feel drops of perspiration on my forehead and moisture dripping down my back. Each step of the way, each willful choice I made screamed "This is wrong!" But I was dazed by lust, although I had convinced myself that it was love, so I continued driving toward our rendezvous location. I wasn't running away from anything; I was running *to* something, something that Vanessa provided.

As anxious as I was, I felt as though my entire body was experiencing a physical, euphoric "high."

I arrived at our meeting place where Vanessa was waiting for me, and I knocked on the door. She opened the door wide and greeted me warmly, inviting me inside. Stepping through that doorway, I crossed a major line of demarcation, which for me was the point of no return. Although it may have been physically possible to turn back, I had made a conscious decision to have sex with Vanessa. We chitchatted nervously for a few brief moments, then hugged and kissed like high school kids.

We had sex, and it felt great.

Then came the surprise. Both of us looked at each other and reality set in, hitting us hard. *What did we just do? We will never be the same. We will never be the people we were prior to this day.*

We were together for less than an hour or so. Without stating it aloud, we both sensed that something had changed as a result of having sex with each other. We were different.

Later that day I felt a strong sense of conviction about my actions. I prayed, "Oh, God, forgive me, please!"

We didn't pray together, but I later learned that Vanessa did something similar. I felt certain she loved God, so she was not callously casting off her faith by having intercourse with me. We were two broken people who connected, naively thinking we could become whole by having sex together.

When we talked later, we said, "That was fantastic, but it's never going to happen again. We are friends, but we can't cross the line, moving from friends to lovers—adulterous lovers."

We agreed, and I was even more emphatic. "Look, I know we have strong emotions, but we know this is wrong. We can't do it."

When I returned home to Shannon that night, I acted as though it were just a normal day. As far as I could tell, she didn't detect anything amiss. We were already operating on autopilot, so we simply went through our routines. As I slipped into our bed that night, I thought, *I can't believe what I have done.* I stared up at the ceiling, and before long, my thoughts moved to, *I hope nobody ever finds out. Jim Bakker, Jimmy Swaggart, Jim Pourteau . . . we're all screwups.*

True to our word, Vanessa and I did not see each other alone again. At least not right away. We did, however, send text messages back and forth, every hour.

"Are you okay?" I asked.

"Yeah, yeah, I'm alright," she said.

"Okay, good."

We reset our moral compasses for a few days, but when we saw each other at rehearsal on Thursday, all the emotions overwhelmed me again. Everyone went out to eat together afterward, and I sensed an awkwardness I had never known. I also felt as though our sexual attraction had intensified, not lessened. The draw to Vanessa was even stronger. I felt better around her.

Not surprisingly, perhaps, it was a whole lot easier to cross those moral lines the second time than it had been the first time. Then the third and fourth times were easier yet. Before long, I compartmentalized my beliefs, lied to myself so much, and convinced myself that Shannon didn't care about me. I justified my actions so completely that I could actually leave rehearsal or a vibrant church service and afterward go have sex with Vanessa.

Didn't I know better? Did my conscience not bother me? Yes. But my conscience was dulled by desire; my intellect was overcome by my emotions. As long as Vanessa made me feel significant and wanted, I could avoid learning who I really was myself.

PART V

EXPOSED

CHAPTER 20

BE STILL AND KNOW

Tempted as she was to do so, Shannon never said a word to Keith about her suspicions that Vanessa and I were having an affair. Part of her reticence to speak to him was that she didn't want to hurt me, and part of her not speaking the truth was she wanted to protect Keith.

Keith often said to Shannon, "I wish Vanessa would love me the way you love Jim."

Shannon never responded with anything negative about Vanessa. Instead, she attempted to turn the conversation in a different direction. "I hope I die before Jim," Shannon said, "because I wouldn't want to live without him."

Keith shook his head in amazement. "I wish my wife felt that way about me," he said.

Nobody in our church of three thousand people said a word to lift the curtain on the sordid theater taking place right in front of them.

When Vanessa's grandmother died, Vanessa was distraught, so during the funeral visitation, I tried to stay close to her to console and hold her in ways that were acceptable in front of others from our church. Shannon noticed and tried to step in between us.

"I'm worried about Vanessa," I said to Shannon. "She's been crying all day and hasn't eaten a thing."

"Oh, are you concerned about her?" Shannon asked. "I'll get her a snack. I'll get her something to eat."

I rolled my eyes in disgust.

Once in the car, I looked at Shannon and groused, "Why are you so concerned about Vanessa now?"

She looked back at me, her beautiful eyes seared into my heart, but she didn't say a thing.

• • • • •

I was on the platform almost every service at Liberty, and ordinarily, Shannon accompanied me to church, despite her growing suspicions and frustration. One Sunday morning, as I finished getting ready, she stated simply, "I'm not going to church today. I just can't do it."

I didn't argue with her. I didn't even ask her why. I didn't even care. I simply said, "Okay," and walked out the door.

In our church with so many people and multiple services, the congregation did not expect to see the pastor's wife sitting on the front row for every service, listening to her husband, so I knew that few people would notice Shannon's absence. And in some ways, it was almost easier for me if I did not have to look out from the platform and see my wife in the audience. Moreover, with Shannon not in the sanctuary, I worried less that "today might be the day when the volcano erupts and she explodes in the church." I had studied psychology enough to know that when someone of Shannon's personality type comes to the end of the rope and finally blows his or her top, the results are often irreparable.

Apparently, Shannon felt the same way. She later said, "I couldn't stand to look at either one of them. Both Vanessa and Jimmy were up there on the stage, worshipping, and then Jimmy stood up and preached about God, family, and love. I couldn't watch it or listen to that any longer. They sickened me."

Unknown to me, Shannon did speak to Karen, my stepmom, who loved Shannon as her own daughter and who Shannon always regarded as her true mother-in-law. Shannon confided to Karen, "I think Jimmy is having an affair with a woman from our church. I don't know for sure, I don't have the proof, but it sure seems that way."

Karen replied softly, "I don't know what's going on with my son. I love him. All I can tell you is that God keeps telling me, 'Be still and know that I am God.'" This was a Scripture, Psalm 46:10, the very message that God seemed to be impressing on Shannon's spirit.

Shannon took those words to heart and did her best to comply with them. She pondered things in her heart, prayed, read books that she hoped might help her understand our marriage, and continued to believe for the best. She did not castigate me or rail against me. "I just wanted it all to stop," she said later. "I wanted things to go back to hearing Jimmy say, 'I love you' every morning and evening."

But it wasn't happening.

Then came the day in early autumn when Shannon and I were in our home and I shocked her with what I perceived to be the truth.

She was sitting in a chair in our sun-washed formal living room when I walked in and said, "I don't love you anymore. I feel like I'm ready to give up everything. I'm willing to walk away from the twenty years of ministry. I'm in love with someone else."

Shannon was shocked. "What?"

I looked directly at Shannon. "I love you," I said, "but I don't love you like a husband should love a wife."

She later told me that my stepmom's scriptural reminder went through her mind: "Be still and know that I am God."

"I don't understand," Shannon said. "How can you say that? How can you do this?"

"I think I love someone else . . . and not you," I admitted. I didn't tell her that someone was Vanessa, one of her best friends.

On a Sunday morning a few weeks later, while I was at church, Shannon stayed home alone. She spotted my briefcase and decided, almost on a whim, to look through it.

Within my briefcase, Shannon found several cards from Vanessa written to me. The cards expressed statements such as "I love you" and "I can't wait till we can get married and have children together."

As she read the cards, Shannon's eyes welled with tears. The discovery of those cards, confirming her fears, crushed her. Beyond my blatant betrayal of our marriage vows, Shannon was decimated by Vanessa's bubbly assumption that she and I would conceive children and raise a family together. After all that Shannon had gone through in her attempts to have children—the numerous stressful doctor's visits over the years, the emotional upheaval of losing three babies through miscarriages, the multiple injections for in vitro treatments, and the enormous amount of money we spent trying to get pregnant—here was another woman, a woman Shannon had trusted, anticipating the joy of having children with me.

Shannon later admitted, "The words in those cards stabbed deeply into my heart. I felt like an abject failure."

Shannon called my stepmom and through her tears said, "I found the proof. I know they really are having an affair." She told my stepmom about the cards she had found in my briefcase. They wept together and again embraced the promise, "Be still and know that I am God."

Shannon told nobody else about what she had found—not her mother or father, not her friends, not even me.

We still slept together in the same bed, but I didn't touch Shannon. I showed her no love or physical affection and few words of conversation. We were truly sleeping single in a king-sized bed.

Somewhere in this nightmare, I had begun drinking heavily, not simply a glass of wine at dinner or a casual glass of bourbon with friends. I was drinking to get drunk—and succeeding. One night, around two o'clock in the morning while I was in a drunken stupor, Shannon left me lying asleep in our bed; she got up and slipped into her car. She drove away from the house and found a place where she could safely pull off on the side of the road. She sat there for the longest time, crying and screaming at God. "Why is this happening, God?" she wailed. She later said, "I realized that if something happened to me out there in the middle of the night, Jimmy wouldn't even know. He wouldn't care. I had no one to talk to . . . so I just cried out to God."

Years later, someone asked Shannon, "Why would you even go back to your house?"

Shannon's answer then and now was, "I didn't want to be a failure. I didn't want our marriage to end in divorce like my parent's had. I wasn't an unfeeling, emotionless 'saint.' I did all the things that any woman in my situation would do," Shannon replied. "I yelled, screamed, cussed a litany of profanity, but I never did it in front of Jimmy. I somehow knew that if I were to throw a tantrum and directed that sort of response toward Jimmy, he would be disgusted with me and would walk off. Or he would respond in kind or worse, and he would leave. Bottom line, as irrational as it was, I didn't want that to happen."

Although she didn't know it at the time, she was absolutely correct. I had an estranged mind; I was already disconnected from her. So if she had railed against me or lamented about how deeply she felt the pain, her actions would have been counterproductive. She would have brought on the exact opposite response from me that she hoped to produce by revealing her pain. To me, she would have appeared pathetic and would have driven me away. I would have bolted because, at that point, I didn't care. I had already emotionally disconnected. For me to have responded positively to any emotional outbursts from Shannon would have required that I cared.

Sorry to say, I didn't.

So after venting to God, Shannon eventually drove back home that night and, emotionally drained, quietly slipped into bed.

Had she not told me about the incident later, I might never have known she was gone.

CHAPTER 21

LIVING WITH THE LIE

For the first time in my life, I wanted to celebrate my birthday as it approached in October of that year. I had experienced few birthday parties during my childhood with no positive memories from any of them, so I had stopped celebrating my birthday by the time I was thirteen. I never knew if any of my family members would show up at a birthday party for me, so why inflict more pain? Yet, for some reason, when I was immersed in an affair with Shannon's friend, I wanted to have a birthday party.

Shannon organized a birthday party for me and sent out the invitations, most of which went to people in our church congregation, including Vanessa and Keith. During the party, Vanessa was overly expressive, frequently touching my hand and arm right in front of Keith and Shannon. I could tell that Shannon noticed, and I guessed that other people did too. "You need to stop," I whispered to Vanessa. "There are a lot of other people here." Even while I was opening presents, Shannon stood opposite me, and Vanessa again sidled in right next to me, handing me each present. I had grown so accustomed to her being close to me, I didn't even notice her inappropriate moves.

But Shannon did.

On the card from Keith and her, Vanessa had written, "Happy Birthday, Jim. We love you. Keith and Vans."

When Shannon saw it, she vented, "When did she go from Vanessa to Vans?" she asked, right in front of everybody.

I smiled at Vanessa but didn't respond to Shannon's question.

On one occasion, Shannon and I were home alone and she wanted to have sex with me. I refused. "I can't do it," I told her bluntly. "I would be cheating on Vanessa."

"What!" Shannon was devastated but held her words.

Only one time did Shannon lose it. My stepmom and dad were visiting, and I talked about Vanessa the entire time. Shannon's blood began to boil. When we both were in the bedroom, she beat on my chest and screamed, "And you are supposed to be a minister?"

Pleaser that she was, she later apologized for hitting me.

That same month, our church women's group asked Shannon to speak at their retreat. She reluctantly agreed. The night before Shannon's early morning speaking engagement, Vanessa and Keith came over to our house. Shannon went to bed early because she wanted to be rested, but Keith, Vanessa, and I stayed up late and were loudly talking and laughing in our TV room.

The conversation turned to all the gifts over the years that I had given to Shannon. "I don't understand why she is so ungrateful," I complained. "I don't know what else she wants. She has diamonds and a Rolex watch. She has everything she could want in life." I went into the bedroom where Shannon was trying to sleep and brought out her jewelry box to show Vanessa and Keith all the expensive baubles I had given to Shannon.

"Look at all these things I've bought for her," I said. "None of which she really appreciated, I might add," I told them. "She doesn't give a crap about this stuff!" The three of us all laughed uproariously. "I can't make her happy," I said. "She doesn't care. She doesn't treat me well."

Vanessa nodded her head vigorously while Keith stared at me quizzically.

Just then, Shannon came out from the bedroom with an agitated expression on her face, her hands on her hips. "I have to get up early tomorrow morning to minister, and you are keeping me awake!" she huffed.

Shannon noticed her jewelry box in front of Vanessa. "And what are you doing with my jewelry?" she asked.

Vanessa and I laughed, and Keith placed his hand on his cheek and looked away silently. Shannon turned on her heels and went back into the bedroom, closing the door much harder than necessary.

During her talk the next morning, she compared our human hearts to an apple. "We look pretty on the outside," she said, "but we sin and rot from the inside." She wasn't throwing darts toward anyone else. If anything, she was being overly introspective and critical about herself.

Afterward, Shannon stood down front and began crying in the church multipurpose area. A woman named Rebecca who had attended the event noticed Shannon and slipped up next to her to comfort her. "I know you are upset," Rebecca said, "and if you ever want to talk, please come to me. I'm available to you."

Shannon thanked her but did not confide any reason for her tears.

That same night, Shannon went to Vanessa and apologized to her. "I'm sorry I have been so mean to you," Shannon said. She felt badly for the way she had been treating Vanessa lately and that she had cooled in their friendship.

Vanessa hugged Shannon but didn't admit to any wrongdoing.

• • • • •

Once, when I was not at home, Shannon went through the house and grabbed anything of mine that she could get her hands on. She gathered clothes, pictures, books, and other personal items and threw them all out in the backyard. "I hate this! I bought this for him," she yelled as she tossed more of my belongings outside. "I can't believe he is doing this!"

After a while, Shannon said to herself, "Well, this is silly! What am I doing? Throwing his stuff out of the house isn't going to hurt Jimmy. And it's sure not helping."

Then, long before I got home, she began feeling remorse for her actions and sheepishly went back outside, retrieved all of my belongings, and replaced them exactly as they were before her outburst. Our dog, Maxwell, watched her with his head tilted as though in bewilderment or amusement. Had she not told me of the incident years later, I might never have known.

• • • • •

Our anniversary was in November, but I purposely did not offer to do anything special with Shannon. Instead, I gave Shannon a thank-you card for our anniversary. Not roses, candy, or a special trip or spa day, not even a "Happy Anniversary" card. I gave her a *thank-you* card that I had specifically chosen. The card said, "Thank you for all the times . . ." and then listed a few generic experiences that any married couple could claim. The text was complimentary but not romantic in any way, platonic but not loving. I didn't want to lead Shannon on by giving her a card saying, "I love you" or "Happy Anniversary to my wife" or any other smarmy, mushy lies that I didn't feel, so I simply purchased a card that said "Thanks."

Along with it, I gave Shannon a dress, one that Vanessa had helped me to pick out for her.

That same month, my grandfather died, so Shannon and I traveled to Louisiana together for the funeral. All the while we were there, we perpetuated the facade that everything was wonderful, that we were the happily married couple that had said "I do" in front of my granddad and many of the same people who had gathered to pay their respects to my grandfather. That was hard, and my emotions threatened to overwhelm me. My granddad was my hero; he was like a father to me. It was even worse because Shannon and Pawpaw were close. I didn't dare think what Pawpaw might have said had he known what was really going on in our marriage. I was ashamed of what my grandfather would have thought of me.

Throughout the visitation and the funeral, Shannon did not hint to anybody that something was wrong in our marriage. Afterward, the out-of-town family members went back to the casino/hotel complex at Lake Charles where we were staying, and Shannon talked briefly with my brother, Marcus. She had known Marcus as long as she had known me, so she confided in him that she thought I might be having an affair.

Marcus listened to Shannon's surprising revelation but offered no suggestions. Nevertheless, before Shannon and I left Louisiana, he took me aside and said, "She's on to you. She mentioned to me that you are having an affair with someone."

I went straight back to Shannon and said, "I can't believe you would think you could share something like that with my own brother and that I would not find out." I didn't address the fact of the affair but instead ripped Shannon for thinking that she could find compassion in Marcus.

When we returned from Louisiana, Shannon was increasingly suspicious, but other than the cards in my briefcase, she had no direct proof of my improper relationship with Vanessa. Never did she look me in the eyes and say, "Tell me the truth. Are you having an affair with Vanessa?"

It's doubtful whether I would have told her the truth anyhow. So we continued living as though everything were normal. We went to Christmas parties, we went to events with Vanessa and Keith, and in public, we functioned as though everything in our marriage was fine.

We traveled to Virginia to spend Christmas with my parents. We treated each other nicely while there. Once again, by all external appearances, Shannon and I were the happy couple. But we both knew differently. Maybe being around my dad and stepmom evoked feelings of guilt and conviction in me. Whatever the reason, while there, in one of our private moments in the bedroom, I broke down in tears in front of Shannon. I hugged her and held her closely to my chest. "I'm sorry, Shannon," I told her. "I've done some terrible things. I don't think we can go on."

Shannon was amazingly gracious. "Jimmy, don't even tell me what you have done," she spoke softly and kindly. "I don't want to know the details. We can get through this. We can make this work. Let's just move forward."

I reached out and held Shannon's hand as I spoke. "I've done so many bad things. I don't think you can ever forgive me," I said.

"I can forgive you," Shannon answered. "I already have."

Shannon later confided, "I thought we were going to go back to Massachusetts and fix things. I thought Jimmy wanted the same."

That did not turn out to be the case.

CHAPTER 22

EXPOSED!

As soon as we returned to Massachusetts, our newfound hope dissipated, mostly because I made a beeline back to Vanessa. One night, our group went line dancing together, and as usual, Vanessa and I flirtatiously flaunted our "friendship." As we drove home, my conversation with Shannon got hot, and I said horribly mean things to her.

"Why would you want to stay with me?" I practically taunted her. "I don't love you; I don't even like you."

"Jimmy, you can be as mean as you want," Shannon said. "You are not going to push me away."

I took Shannon's courageous words as a challenge and intensified my vehement vitriol.

"We're only married according to a piece of paper," I growled. "We have no kids. Thank God you never had our baby. I'm glad we couldn't have children. You'd have been a terrible mother."

Shannon winced but was undeterred. "Jimmy, I know you are just being mean and trying to push me away," she said. "You are saying these mean things because you want me to hate you, and I am not going to do it. You can be as mean as you want to be, Jimmy, I am not going to go anywhere. I am not going to leave you."

Not that my vicious comments didn't crush her. Shannon thought, *Who is this person? He is not the same person who every morning and evening for the past twenty years has told me that he loves me. What has happened to my husband?*

We got home and went into the house. Shannon was in tears, her heart broken. My heart was cold and hard.

Shannon and I occasionally engaged in strained but amicable conversations all the way from October to December. During those discussions, I tried to convince her that God wanted us to get a divorce so Vanessa and I could be together.

"No, that is not what God wants," Shannon protested. "You know that God says He hates divorce."

"Yes, but sometimes people marry the wrong partners," I attempted to convince her.

She wasn't buying it.

For the most part, Shannon maintained her dignity in front of me, but some days she simply couldn't take any more. On those days when she'd had enough, she found some location away from me and just screamed to God.

Shannon later said, "I knew there was no use in confronting Jimmy. He'd probably just get angry, explode, and leave. I didn't want to push him away more than he already felt I had done. So I simply remained quiet. There were no ground rules for how to operate in this unusual situation. I had no preparation or help regarding what to do. I repeatedly told myself, 'He's a good guy doing a bad thing.'"

Throughout this time, neither Shannon nor I consulted with any other pastor or counselor. Why would I trust other people to help us? My prevailing attitude was, "Everyone will screw you over, one day." We were mired in our own stuff, going nowhere.

• • • • •

Shannon and I had decided to celebrate New Year's Eve by getting all dressed up and going out to dinner with a group of our friends. We hadn't been getting along well that week, but Shannon was excited, nonetheless. Early that evening, as I was getting ready, Vanessa and I texted back and forth, sending each other photographs of the outfits we planned to wear that night.

We went out to a New Year's Eve party and stayed until the ball dropped in Times Square, and we had a good time. We went home and crawled into bed, me on my side, Shannon on hers. I planned to spend New Year's Day watching some football games and preparing my sermon for the upcoming weekend's church services.

That night, about two o'clock in the morning, we were sleeping soundly when my telephone rang. Shannon was lying in bed next to me. I rolled over and reached for the phone. "Hello," I said groggily, trying to brush the sleep out of my eyes. My first thought was that there must be some emergency within the church congregation, that somebody was in trouble.

Somebody was—me!

Vanessa was on the phone. Her voice was frantic and it sounded as though she was crying. "Jimmy! Keith has found out about us. He says he is going to expose us first thing in the morning." Apparently, he had gotten into her phone and had discovered compromising messages between Vanessa and me.

"What? Okay, calm down," I said, sitting up in bed. I was wide awake now. "Tell me what's going on." I could feel Shannon stirring next to me and knew that she was awake and listening.

Vanessa continued sobbing into the phone. "I'm scared. I've locked myself in a room. Keith knows. He knows about us and he is going to tell it to the church leaders tomorrow."

I sighed deeply. "This is good," I said. "I'm glad it is all coming out. I'm tired of hiding everything."

"Jimmy!" Vanessa cried.

"We didn't know how this news was going to get out, but now it has been decided for us," I said.

I talked further to Vanessa and told her that I would see her in the morning. My mind was racing a million miles an hour, so I was barely aware that Shannon was crying and had crawled out of bed. She took a blanket and pillow and went downstairs and curled up on the couch.

Shannon recalls, "I could tell by Jimmy's voice what was going on. Plus, I had found the cards in his briefcase, so I knew they had been having an affair. I was tired and emotionally exhausted, but sleep eluded me for the longest time. When I finally fell asleep, I had a horrible nightmare in which I saw our former pastors warning us and saying that it was my fault, that we should not have gone to the Massachusetts church after all. I woke up crying on the couch."

About that time, as the sun dawned on a new day and a new year, I dressed and went downstairs. I walked over to where Shannon was stirring, sobbing on the couch. "I can't do this anymore," I said to her. "We're getting a divorce. I'm leaving," I said coldly.

Shannon burst out crying and screamed, "I want my dad!" She curled into a fetal position and wept loudly, producing sounds that could only come from a woman whose heart was being crushed.

She was still crying when I walked out the door.

CHAPTER 23

COPING AND CONFLICTED

When your world blows up or falls apart, it is odd how we attempt to cope. For me, I was conflicted. I knew I could not simply run off with Vanessa, as much as we had hinted about doing so. Besides, I still felt some responsibility to inform the church leaders about Vanessa and me and to give them a heads-up about what was likely to happen. I didn't know if Keith had contacted them yet or not, but I had no intention of intercepting or impeding him.

Later that morning, I called Will, the senior pastor at Liberty. It was a Friday morning, New Year's Day, and we had a Saturday night service and a full slate of services scheduled for Sunday, so I knew I had to contact him before word of my affair got out. It was a foregone conclusion to me that I would not be preaching that weekend, that indeed, my preaching days were over.

"Will, bottom line is that I don't love Shannon," I told him. "I haven't loved her for quite a while. We've been having some tough times. I'm leaving her and we'll probably get divorced as soon as possible. I'm in love with Vanessa."

Will was stunned but didn't sound surprised. I knew that he had been struggling with his own marital stress, so apparently he was emotionally prepared for the news.

I told him that I would submit my resignation to the church and give up my ordination license. Will was empathetic but did not try to stop me or talk me out of my actions.

I stayed at a friend's place for a few days. I thought that Keith may call me and want to talk or fight or something, but he never did. Looking back, no doubt he simply put all the pieces together and realized that our affair was not a recent development.

Monday, I met with Will and shared with him more details. Will commiserated and repeatedly said, "I understand, I get it." But he offered no program of repentance and restoration that would help me repent, find forgiveness, and eventually be reinstated as a Christian minister. Nor did I ask him for such or want him to intercede for me. I resigned from the church on Tuesday and then called the denominational headquarters to relinquish my ordination. Within a matter of a few days, everything I had worked to achieve in my life was gone.

The following weekend, Vanessa and I went away together because we didn't want to be in Shrewsbury when the news of our affair was made known to the congregation at Liberty and in town.

After I left her on New Year's Day, Shannon stayed at our house by herself for a month, with her only company our dog, Max. I had told her that I wasn't coming back and to go ahead and sell our beautiful home. "Do whatever you want to do," I told her. "Sell the house for whatever you can get for it."

She expressed no rancor toward me. In fact, as we were collecting items from the spare bedroom, she still had hopes that our marriage might survive. She said to me, "Jimmy, do you think we can make this work?"

"No!" I railed. "You are the dumbest person I know. I'm so glad that we didn't have kids, because I would be stuck with you and I would have had to raise them *and* you."

There was no excuse for me being so despicably mean to her, and the hurt on Shannon's face was palpable. "Okay, if you want to do this, and you don't want to stay with me, fine," she said. "But is your soul okay?"

"What?" I asked. My eternal destiny was the last thing on my mind.

"I don't want you to die and go to hell," she said sweetly. She seemed sincerely concerned about my spiritual condition, worried that my actions and attitudes were causing me to be estranged not only from her but from God.

"Arrgh," I huffed. "Let me alone."

She did.

• • • • •

I guessed that Vanessa would be moving out of her home soon, so I gave her some old furniture stored in our basement—furniture that Shannon's mom had given us—and I remained at my friend's home until I could figure out what to do next. Meanwhile, Shannon was not giving up on us. She continued reading books about marriage. One that was especially meaningful to her was Stormie Omartian's book, *The Power of Prayer to Change Your Marriage*.

The first chapter Shannon read was about infidelity and forgiveness. The author emphasized that we need to forgive others if we expect God to forgive us. "I knew that God was a forgiving God, and He had forgiven me, so I felt that I had to forgive Jimmy," Shannon recalls. "But I also had to forgive my friend, Vanessa. I was hurt and angry with her, but I realized that she was a hurting person as well. No doubt, she had believed that her future with Jimmy would be one of great influence and fruitful ministry."

Although Shannon's heart was broken, she knew she had to pick up the pieces of her life and go back to work. Shannon's birthday on January 14 went unnoticed by me. I didn't even send her a card. When our goddaughter's family learned about my leaving Shannon, they invited her to visit and stay with them in Connecticut for a weekend. They felt so sad for her. They knew how much Shannon enjoyed country music, so one night, to help lift Shannon's spirits, they all went out line dancing together. At the dance club, a man named Frank struck up a conversation with Shannon.

Shannon recalls, "Frank seemed nice, and he was definitely interested in me, but all I could talk with him about was Jimmy and our relationship—not exactly a good way to begin a new friendship."

On one occasion after Shannon and I had engaged in a bitter conversation, she called Frank just to talk to somebody with a listening ear. She was crying and sobbing on the phone, and Frank instantly picked up on her sadness and tried to console her. "I just got in the car," he said. "I'm on my way. I want to come to comfort you."

"No, Frank," she said. "Don't come."

"I'm already in the car," he said.

"No, you can't come here. You can't stay here. I'm still married," Shannon told him.

"Okay, he said. "I won't, but please let me know if you need anything."

• • • • •

Shannon left our former home in the hands of a realtor the second week of February, carrying with her the last remnants of her possessions and memories of our life together, along with our faithful dog. Although my dad's construction business was head-quartered in Texas, my parents were now living in Prince George, Virginia, in a rental home, while Dad worked on a large military development near Fort Lee. Shannon intended to drive to Virginia, stop over at my parents' place, and then go on to Lake Wiley, South Carolina, where she planned to live for a while with her parents.

Her friend, Frank, asked her to stop at his house in Connecticut along her way. "We'll have dinner and can watch a movie," Frank suggested.

"Okay," Shannon said.

As Shannon later recalled, they enjoyed a casual dinner and then talked for a while.

"You can sleep here," said Frank, "and then get up and go in the morning."

He knew Shannon was broken, lonely, and vulnerable, but he was the perfect gentleman and didn't try anything forward with Shannon.

"I'll sleep right here on the couch," Shannon said.

Frank respectfully retreated to the bedroom.

Shannon kept her clothes on and snuggled in on the sofa. She closed her eyes and tried to rest, but sleep would not come. After a while, around two o'clock in the morning, she called out to Frank. "I'm just going to go."

Frank returned to the living room. "Shannon, it is the middle of the night, and the weather outside is awful," Frank said. "Wouldn't you rather stay here and drive during the daylight?"

"No," she said. "I can't sleep, so I'm going to go. Don't worry. I'll be okay."

Shannon had told Frank that I was with Vanessa, so before Shannon left that night, Frank offered to attend her brother's wedding—an event for which I was to serve as the officiant. "If you are single by then, I'll be glad to go with you," he said.

Shannon let him know that she appreciated his friendship, but that was as far as she was willing to go.

"I know you are hurt," Frank said. "I'm not going to push you. Just call me if you ever need me."

So in the wee hours of the morning, Shannon and our dog got in the car and headed out from Connecticut to Virginia, about ten hours away, driving her mini-Cooper through the snow. They arrived at my mom and dad's home later that afternoon, the same home where I was temporarily staying.

That was awkward, especially since Shannon knew that I was now with Vanessa. But even though I had adamantly told Shannon I didn't want anything to do with her and to leave me alone, we still had to interact with each other. For instance, our home had not yet sold, and she had large items that she needed to take to South Carolina for her clerical work.

So in mid-February, I loaded items from a storage unit into my pickup truck. With Shannon following in her Mini-Cooper, my stepmom, Karen, and I drove the bulky items to Shannon's parents' home south of Charlotte, just over the South Carolina border. Her parents were not at home when we arrived because they were in California attending the funeral of her stepbrother. We walked into the cold, vacant house, and I helped my wife unload the large pieces from the truck, as well as her suitcases and personal items. Before Karen and I left town, we took Shannon to get something to eat and then back to the house to drop her off all by herself.

Knowing that it was going to be a tough day for Shannon, my parents had prepared a special gift bag filled with candy and treats for her. I noticed the red cards and candies, and it was only then that I realized that it was Valentine's Day.

Happy Valentine's Day, Shannon.

I drove off as quickly as possible.

My stepmom and I traveled back to Virginia. Now that our home in Massachusetts was on the market, I had moved in with my parents as a forty-year-old. The spartan eleven-by-eleven-foot bedroom was tight, with barely enough space for a bed with no headboard. I bought some cardboard drawers to hold my socks and shirts. Although I appreciated my parents' hospitality, I felt as though I was living in a college dormitory. This was a far cry from the beautiful home I had left, but my situation did not discourage me. I was convinced that my "new life" with Vanessa was about to unfold and everything would soon be good again.

I talked with my parents about my future. I wanted to start a new business with them, but my dad cautioned me, "People do crazy stuff under pressure." I knew he loved Shannon, but his words made sense to me. I talked myself into thinking that Shannon may try to take my business in our eventual divorce proceedings, which was ludicrous. That would go totally contrary to her personality.

Nevertheless, Shannon did have to start life all over again in a new location, starting work again, with no financial resources to speak of to support her. Despite losing our marriage and everything we owned materially, Shannon never threw things in my face as some spouses do when their marriage is disintegrating. I'd heard of one woman who said, "I went outside and banged my head against the car windshield until blood literally ran down my face, and my husband still left." No kidding. Sometimes people think that nagging helps or that attempts to show how much an affair has caused pain will evoke compassion and cause the spouse to return. Quite the contrary; such behavior usually pushes a wayward spouse further away.

Shannon did not do those sorts of things. She never lashed out; she never spoke hatefully or spitefully to me. She didn't whine, nor did she speak negatively to anyone else about me. Oftentimes, when a couple's marriage is in trouble, one or both partners will "poison the well" by making derogatory remarks about their partner to another person. Unless those comments are made within the confidentiality of a private counseling session, even if the statements are true and well deserved, they are almost always counterproductive, especially if the couple gets back together. Those negative statements are still "out there," maintaining a life of their own. They tend to resurface at the most inconvenient times.

Shannon did not do that. She never poisoned the well by tearing me down to other people. Instead, she prayed. She believed. She trusted God, even when she could no longer trust me.

CHAPTER 24

RUNNING FROM GOD— RUNNING TO GOD

I continued to treat Shannon despicably. When I last spoke to her, I told her, "Stop telling me that you love me. Quit texting me. Leave me alone!"

So she did. She didn't call, text, write, or attempt to communicate with me at all. She did the smart thing. Although I didn't know it at the time, she took my stepmom's advice about believing God and being still. Shannon continued to maintain an amazing calmness, despite the circumstances. To her credit, she said little to anybody else about our marriage and simply prayed that somehow, some way, God would bring me to my senses.

If He was going to do that, He'd have to catch me.

I had not attended church for months. That was so unusual for me since I had been a regular church attender most of my life. But after my relationship with Vanessa was exposed in Shrewsbury, neither she nor I felt comfortable in returning to church. I wasn't interested in hearing from God or some preacher who claimed to represent Him. Indeed, I was convinced that the moment I walked inside a sanctuary, everyone there would see a scarlet letter A on my chest and would want nothing to do with me. Of course, I foolishly felt that was God's fault, even though I knew better. Nevertheless, I avoided church services.

More than social interaction, however, I missed being in the presence of God that I had grown accustomed to experiencing in church. So I decided to risk finding a church in Virginia that I could attend. But not just any church. I wanted to go someplace where I could blend in with the crowd. Ironically, for most of my life, I had attempted to avoid feeling invisible, but now I wanted to be unnoticed.

Before I went back to church, I took a picture of me standing outside my pickup truck and sent it to Vanessa. I had justified my actions with her and convinced myself that I was in love with her. And as strange as it may sound, I believed that, contrary to His stated Word, God was going to bless our adulterous relationship and that we would someday be back in the ministry together. *Maybe God had that in mind all along, that we were to be together*, I mused. As strange as it seemed, for all the tension and drama going on around me, when I was with Vanessa, I felt peace. Or at least what I thought was peace.

How weird was that? But when a person is living in delusion, such contradictions seem rational and completely logical. Both Vanessa and I thought that we could build a life together and maybe even have some future ministry. Psychologists call this cognitive dissonance, when a person is acting in contradiction to his or her values. When what they are doing intersects with the person's values, it creates disharmony within, even if the individual cannot understand the reason for their discontentment, even if it is the good intersecting with the bad.

So I told Vanessa, "I can't explain it, but I've decided I want to go to church. I can't deny God; I know He's there. I can't explain what's going on with us, but I'm going back to church."

I now understand that God was drawing me back to Himself, but at the time, I thought it was my idea.

I didn't want to go to an Assemblies of God church because I was relatively well-known within those groups. Nor did I want to go to one of the hundreds of smaller churches in the area where I was living, because I was certain to stand out as a newcomer. There would be too many questions—questions I didn't care to answer.

I found Colonial Heights Baptist Church, in Colonial Heights, Virginia, a congregation about the size of the one I had left in Massachusetts. I had never been there previously, but I chose it for my first attempt to reconnect because it seemed similar in size to the place I had left. I felt sure I could slip inside the sanctuary and not be conspicuous.

I purposely arrived a few minutes late, after the service had already begun. That way, I figured, I could avoid greeting people or being greeted.

An usher saw me, however, and offered to find me a seat down close to the front.

"No thanks," I said. "I just want to sit in the back and check things out." I slipped inside the sanctuary and sat down on a seat in the back row.

The service was a rather typical, traditional Baptist approach, with music led by a song leader up front and authentic biblical preaching. In truth, it was not the type of worship service to which I was accustomed, but as I sat through the service, I sensed the presence of God. The realization flooded over me that for the first time in a long, long time, I could simply be myself. I didn't have to perform; I wasn't worried about living up to anyone's expectations

of me. It struck me that I had not simply *attended* and participated in a Sunday morning worship service like this for more than
twenty years. I was always the guy up front, encouraging other
people. Now the mask was off, and I could come into God's presence merely as a needy person wanting to experience His grace.

Since becoming a Christian as a teenager, I had tried to be a
good role model for others. I fretted that it all depended on me. If
I didn't present an upbeat impression, other people in the church
would be discouraged. If I didn't raise my hands in worship to the
Lord, they probably wouldn't either. I felt that as a leader, I had
a responsibility to point people to God, regardless of how I felt
within or what I was personally experiencing. I came to feel that
the church services depended on my external behavior or else they
would be ineffective. I not only preached but sat in the front row
like a monkey on display. I genuinely wanted other people to see
God by looking through me. In the process, I unwittingly took on
myself a load that no human being can possibly bear. Only God's
Spirit can do those things, not me.

Now, as I sat in the back row of the Baptist church, I could just
be there with God. I didn't have to be "the guy." I was anonymous,
except to God.

I don't know what the preacher spoke about, nor do I remember
any of the songs they sang. I just sat there all by myself, listening—
and I cried.

It felt really good.

After the service, I didn't talk with anyone. I quickly got in
my truck and left. I called Vanessa on the way home. "It was really
powerful," I told her. "I was overwhelmed emotionally, sensing the
presence of God."

"I'm glad you enjoyed the church service," she said, "but I'm
not ready for that. I haven't been back to church since . . . well, you
know . . ."

"Yeah, I understand," I said. "But something just seemed right about being there."

I realized that in my absence, God had not abandoned me. Despite all my ranting and running, He was still steady, and as hard as I had tried to push Him away, He had been there all the time, waiting for me to seek Him. I remembered the message of Scripture, that even when we are faithless, God remains faithful to us. Everything that I knew about God said, "While we were yet sinners," as the apostle Paul wrote, "Christ died for us," paying the price for our sins, making a way that we could be forgiven by, reconciled to, and reinstated with God.

But somehow, I had lost the awareness of that truth. Going back to church was a helpful first step toward inner healing for me.

"It's going to be okay," I told Vanessa. "I don't think God hates me."

Vanessa seemed to understand what I was saying, but she didn't offer to jump on board with me. She was still living in the same town but had not returned to our former church since people knew her role as one of the worship leaders. She and Keith had separated by now and were headed toward a divorce. So she stayed in isolation, away from the place where she might have found spiritual encouragement—and she seemed okay with that. I hoped that she might see things differently and develop a desire to attend church again, but I understood her reticence.

On the other hand, I felt compelled to get back into a regular church routine. I genuinely missed meeting with a bunch of other believers, as cracked and broken as all Christians—even the best Christians—truly are.

I thought, *I need to do this. I want to attend church, but I need to let the pastor know where I'm coming from. If he knows more about me, he may be uncomfortable with me being there.* I called the church and made an appointment to meet with the pastor, Randall Hahn.

We met in his office and I introduced myself. "I want you to know that I am coming to your church, just in case . . ." I paused, took a breath, and blurted, ". . . just in case somebody recognizes me, knows my past, and gets upset that I'm attending your services."

The friendly pastor, who I guessed to be around my age, looked at me quizzically but didn't interrupt, so I explained. "I am a former pastor," I began, "and I left my wife for another woman. We're currently still married but will probably get divorced.

"I wanted you to know that. I don't want anything; I'm not looking for anybody. But if you don't mind, I'd like to attend this church for a while. I'm not going to join or volunteer for anything, I just want to be here and sit in the back. I need a place where I can heal. I need to get right."

The pastor was moved with compassion and responded graciously, "You come as you are and be a part of us. Thank you for meeting with me. I'm not worried about you being here. I'm glad you are. Please know we will help any way we can." The pastor seemed like a genuinely good, godly, and empathetic man. He didn't castigate me or condemn me to hell; nor did he condone my affair with Vanessa. He simply accepted me as I was, and he cared. We prayed together and I left.

I attended that Baptist church for a month or more. Each week, I slipped in inconspicuously and sat in the back. I met a few people but purposely avoided lengthy conversations with anyone. Perhaps, most importantly, I felt no fear.

Even though the worship style was not my favorite, that Baptist church was a tremendous encouragement to me. It was God's way of helping me to feel less apprehensive about returning not only to church but to Him. It was a safe place, a place of transition, a place I needed.

About six weeks later, I went to a movie, and as I entered the theater, I noticed a sign announcing that a church also met there.

The pastor was a young guy named Brian Briggs. He had had a dream about that theater two years earlier indicating to him that he was supposed to start a church there. He had prayed about it for a while, and he and his wife and a few believers started a new church in the theater. They named the ministry Destination.

The first time I heard him speak, his blunt message hit me: "You folks need to know that this is who we are," he said. "Jesus says that we are fishers of men. We are not a cruise ship; we are a fishing vessel. On a cruise ship, there are a few people working and a lot of people being served. On a fishing vessel, everybody works."

Pastor Briggs continued, "If you want to be a part of this group, you are welcome, but please understand, everybody here works, everyone serves. Oh, sure, you can come here all you want and watch and listen, but you can't claim this as your *church* unless you are serving and putting your money where your mouth is. We will love you, and we'll help you, but either you are part of the mission or you are not."

Brian's concept of a church resonated with me. The pastor wasn't implying that we can work our way to heaven; rather, he was saying that, as Christians, we ought to be helping other people. I understood that it is impossible to work our way into God's good graces, His presence, or His favor, but I had seen and heard too many people—myself included—who separated what they supposedly believed from how they lived. Brian was laying it on the line, and I liked what I heard.

"On a cruise ship, everyone wears their finest outfits, their fancy swimwear, and color-coordinated everything, so they can sit and be served," Pastor Brian continued. "Here, you will see people with tattoos, with piercings, some dressed in all sorts of strange clothing, everything from suits to T-shirts. In fact, some people know us as the T-shirt church, and that's okay with us. God is looking at your heart, not what label is on your clothing. Fish stink, and when you are fishing, you will probably smell like fish."

As I listened, I thought, *I'm home.*

I attended Destination again the following week, and the message was similar. The next week, I made an appointment to meet with Pastor Brian at a Panera Bread. He did not know me, but we had some mutual friends. I sat across from him and told him my story, and he listened with apparent empathy.

"I don't want to be a pastor," I told him. "I won't ever be a pastor again, I don't want to teach, but if you will allow me, I'd like to help you. Is there somewhere I can do something behind the scenes, a place where I won't run into people? I'll do anything, carry stuff, set up chairs, sweep the floors, any way I can help."

"What?" Pastor Brian seemed surprised at my offer. "You're a former pastor and you want to set up chairs?"

"Yeah, anything. I just want to serve somehow."

The following week when I went to Destination, Brian introduced me to the children's pastor, and I helped set up chairs for the kids. I wore a church name tag, but nobody recognized my name.

A few weeks later, Pastor Brian set up another meeting with me. He had done some checking regarding my background. "Dude, we need help," he said. "Based on what I've heard about you, this is your forte, helping a church go from next to nothing to a new level of significance. We need your sort of expertise."

I appreciated Brian's kind words, but I remained reticent. "I don't want to be in the ministry again," I confessed. "I'm not sure I can handle the pressure, and I'm still recovering from a big mess. I don't know if I'm the right guy for you. Maybe I'm not supposed to be involved in your ministry."

"Don't worry about it, man," Pastor Brian said. "I believe you are gifted and can help us. Give it a shot."

I reluctantly agreed to act as a consultant and do a review of the entire church. I recruited some outside "secret shoppers" to visit the church and give their first impressions. Then I wrote a review about what visitors to the church experienced and how their impressions could be improved.

The church leaders loved it.

"Is there any way you can help us develop this team?" Pastor Brian asked.

I thought about it for a few moments and then heard myself reply, "Yeah, I will help you to train your staff and volunteers."

I was still working in construction and had my own consulting and team-building business, but I soon found myself spending more time with Brian than in my own business. Thanks to Brian's grace-filled attitude and his dedicated team of coworkers, the church grew exponentially. We went to multiple services, then developed another campus in addition to the theater location. Before long, we were doing six services each weekend.

I no longer considered myself a pastor, but God was not going to let me fall through the cracks.

CHAPTER 25

BREAKUP BREAKDOWN

After my affair became public and I had walked out on Shannon, my immediate intention was to get divorced and marry Vanessa as soon as possible, assuming that she would divorce Keith. But when I moved to Virginia, I was told that the state had a one-year waiting period following divorce before a person could remarry. I didn't dig any deeper than that, but I figured that as soon as the year had elapsed, Vanessa and I would move forward.

What I did not know was that the Virginia statute applied only to divorced spouses with children. Spouses with kids had to wait a year before remarrying; spouses without children could marry any time. But I continued under the illusion that I could not remarry for at least another year.

Somewhere Shannon must have been smiling.

Meanwhile, in March of that year after our slow-burn infatuation with each other turned into a full-blown affair, Vanessa and I broke up. It all happened rather quickly.

"Jim, I can't do this anymore," she told me. I was a different man than she thought. She had begun to reassess her Christian values and began noticing the flaws in me. Vanessa had fallen in love with me because she witnessed my love for Shannon and my love for God. She knew that these were the two relationships that had been most important to me for most of my life, and I had abandoned both of those. Perhaps she realized that I wasn't even the person she thought she was getting. Ironically, in breaking up with me, Vanessa commented, "You and Shannon need to be together. You two are right for each other."

My head was spinning again. In about a two-month period, I had gone from being "in love" with Vanessa, thinking I was going to have everything I wanted in life with this young woman, to her breaking up with me. I was in the pit of despair. Vanessa quit talking to me completely and blocked me from contacting her by phone. I was devastated. In addition to my dreams of "happily ever after" being dashed by Vanessa's departure and the accompanying feelings of rejection, I also had to face the fact that I had contributed to the eventual divorce of two of my best friends. Then there was the scandal at the church and the dishonor I had brought to the Lord's name. All of that produced a load of grief and personal guilt.

I tried to find satisfaction in a variety of ways, none of which worked. I had always struggled with feelings of insignificance, but I had no idea how to address the core issues, so I simply tried to meet the emotional needs. I dated a few women, and I enjoyed taking a risk. But the moment a woman became enamored with me or the relationship turned serious, I was done. I had obtained all that I wanted; it seemed that I had found significance for the moment yet still felt unfulfilled. The futility of dating as an adult was frustrating.

I was working with a construction crew, going through an empty house my crew had built for the military in Fort Lee. As I was alone with my thoughts, checking off a punch list of repairs that needed done in an upstairs bedroom, suddenly the weight of my actions and the affair's ramifications overwhelmed me. The affair was over and everything was lost—Shannon, my reputation, my livelihood, everything. Gone. I was a totally different person with no idea what I was going to do with the rest of my life.

I collapsed in a heap on the floor, my hard hat bouncing off, the radio attached to my belt coming unhinged. I simply laid on the floor for the longest time.

Finally, I heard one of my coworkers, Jose, a large Mexican fellow who had previously been a California drug-runner for the cartel. Jose had gotten his life straightened out and now ran a dry wall crew. He and I had become close friends, and Jose often referred to himself as "the third Pourteau brother."

Jose had come looking for me, calling out in his Hispanic accent, "Hey, Jimmy. Jimmy!"

Jose turned the corner and walked into the bedroom. "Hey, Jimmy," he said, and then saw me sprawled out on the floor, with tears in my eyes and streaming down my face. "Oh, Jimmy," he said. "I'll see you *later.*" And he left!

I slowly picked myself up and wiped the tears off my face. I knew I had to get my life together . . . somehow.

• • • • •

Shannon and I talked occasionally. Our conversations were amicable but not in any way conciliatory. Mostly we talked about the sluggish real estate market and the lack of movement in trying to sell our home in Massachusetts. I had no illusions about us getting back together, and as far as I knew, neither did she.

In addition to my construction job, I was still working part-time as a basketball referee, officiating both high school and NCAA collegiate games and staying busy. In many ways, working as a referee was tremendously helpful for me. Besides giving me something to do, the exercise was good for helping to relieve stress and to pull me out of my despair. I loved being on the court, hearing the roar of the crowds in the gymnasiums, and because I was one of only three guys wearing the black and white stripes, my role gave me a sense that I was still in control of some parts of my life.

• • • • •

After it became public knowledge that I had gotten involved in a sexual affair and committed adultery, several friends from our church asked, "Why didn't you talk to me?"

Yeah, right, I thought.

I grappled with a difficult paradox. On the one hand, I believed that the only way to be real as a person, healthy and whole emotionally, was to know God and live the way He has instructed. On the other hand, as a Christian, I was taught to adopt the facade, to maintain an impression of having life all together, even if you don't—no, *especially* if you don't. Even if I wanted to be authentic, I couldn't be without risking the acceptance of my Christian family members and friends. I had to look and sound good. True confidentiality was nonexistent. If I confessed my sins to someone, as the Bible teaches, there was always a fear that my vulnerability would come back to haunt me.

Although I didn't spew my anger all over my well-meaning friends, the truth was that I didn't dare speak to anyone about slouching toward an affair. Why would I? My first spiritual "family" had tried to destroy me, so who could I trust?

Far better to shut my mouth, keep my feelings inside, and absorb the hurt, anger, pain, and shame. So that's what I did.

Ironically, when I finally did attempt to talk to someone about the emotional anger I harbored, he was a pill-pitching nut job.

Keep in mind, I was taught in my faith that if you had diabetes, cancer, or some other physical malady, it was okay to go to a doctor. But if you struggled with anxiety or depression, that was *spiritual*, so you likely needed to pray more. Or if you were really down and discouraged, you may need to be delivered from demonic oppression.

The church ministers meant well, but sometimes they missed the obvious. Some people don't need demons cast out of them. They need their bodies to be chemically balanced.

Consequently, I prayed, "God, please help me!" I often prayed for things that I felt were wrong in my life, yet nothing happened. I grew up thinking that medication was wrong, so for years I never sought help for my serotonin deficiency. Truth is, I'm not sure I knew I had a physical malady. I just knew my emotions could turn from hot to cold almost instantly, especially if someone stepped on one of my hot-button triggers such as abandonment or insignificance.

I had studied Christian counseling and read multitudes of books by authors such as Jay Adams, Larry Crabb, and Tim Keller. I also counseled numerous individuals and couples over the years, but I had never been a patient or met with a clinical, therapeutic type of counselor myself.

But shortly after Shannon and I separated, I experienced a panic attack and felt as though I was losing my mind. It was brutal, the worst sensation I had ever felt. My body trembled, my hands shook, my face glistened with perspiration, and my heart raced and throbbed in my chest with such a vengeance I thought I was having a heart attack.

Rather than seeking counsel, I found a doctor I thought might be able to help me—a psychiatrist. I booked an hour-long appointment. When I walked in the psychiatrist's office, I saw a guy who looked like a bespectacled Sigmund Freud; his three-piece suit was rumpled and disheveled, and his hair was all messed up. I thought, *This guy must be super smart, because he can't even get dressed.*

Much to my chagrin, he didn't even have a couch. *What kind of shrink doesn't have a couch?* I wondered. *Am I not supposed to lie down on a couch and tell this guy all my troubles?* Apparently not. The shrink sat behind his desk that was up against a wall and motioned for me to sit down. He talked to me but didn't look at me. After fifteen minutes of gathering my medical history and asking a few questions about my environment, he turned to me and said, "What kind of drug would you like?"

"What?"

I whimsically thought to myself, *I don't know . . . cocaine? I've not tried that. Do you have a menu I could look at?* But apparently the guy was serious.

"Yes, it is obvious that you are dealing with acute depression, so what sort of drug would you like me to prescribe?" he repeated. "Perhaps you have heard about some of the options."

"I don't know," I said. "Aren't you supposed to tell me that?"

I realized that he had no intention of trying to help me with my stuff; he was simply a pill pusher.

I went to another counselor, and he was no better.

For the next six months or so, I fended for myself. Finally, I mustered the courage to seek help again. I scheduled an appointment with a counselor named Godwin for 8:00 a.m. but when I showed up, the counselor was not there. As it turned out, it just happened to be a morning when I had another major panic attack. My face red, my body perspiring profusely, and my heart thumping loudly again, I paced back and forth impatiently watching for Godwin or anyone who might be able to help me.

At about 8:30 a.m., a frumpy-looking guy showed up wearing beat-up shoes, wrinkled khaki pants, a dark shirt with shapes on it, a square-bottomed necktie, and a drab blue sports jacket, with salt-and-pepper hair all the way down to his butt and reeking with a distinct odor of pot.

"James Pourteau?" he asked.

"Yeah!" I growled.

"I'm Godwin. You have an appointment with me today."

"What?" I stepped right up in front of the counselor's face and yelled, "Where the f--- have you been?"

"I'm sorry?" the counselor responded.

I pushed even closer to Godwin's face and continued to vent. "I was here at eight o'clock," I said. "I've been losing my mind, and I'm freaking out right now. I needed someone to talk to, and you come waltzing in here a half hour or more late. And now I'm supposed to trust you?"

"Jim, I'm really sorry," Godwin said. "To be honest with you, I overslept."

"What? You overslept?"

"Hey, man," he said. "All I can tell you is that you have two choices. You can be upset with me and leave, or we can go back and talk and see if there is something I can help you with."

"Fine!" I groused. We went into Godwin's office and we began to talk. Godwin was a most unlikely character, and it took a year or so, but he genuinely helped me. He truly heard me. He didn't try to advise me; he listened and helped me to discover that for most of my life, I had felt abandoned and insignificant. In all of my relationships, from my parents, to friends, to Shannon, the sense of insignificance permeated my life. I had built walls on which I projected an image of whatever I hoped would cause people to accept me and love me—whether it was a sports guy, a youth leader, pastor, or community leader. Otherwise, I feared that I might be rejected.

To this day, I still take medications for depression and serotonin deficiency. The meds don't dope me up, but they balance the serotonin levels in my body. Without making excuses, I can't help but wonder if my life may have been different had I known earlier how the medications could help me to function better.

PART VI

Falling Back in Love

CHAPTER 26

REACHING OUT

Shannon found a church in South Carolina that she felt comfortable attending. She went to church with her mom and dad, and at lunch, she told them, "No matter what happens with Jimmy and me, I still want to live for God."

"That's good," they said. "But stay strong."

They recognized that for most of our married life, Shannon had put me on a pedestal, like a little god. Now she realized that I was not.

She made an appointment with a Christian counselor, but when Shannon told her the story, she was surprised that the counselor did not seem interested in discussing reconciliation. Instead, the counselor emphatically said, "Adultery is your one way out. Your husband committed adultery, and from a biblical and spiritual standpoint, you have a legitimate reason for walking away from the marriage. He's not a very good man, anyway."

Shannon was so disappointed in the counselor's advice that she never went back.

I wish I could say that in my career, this sort of encounter was rare or this kind of advice was an aberration; it is not. All too often, a counselor is so committed to sticking to the letter of the law that he or she neglects the spirit of the biblical truth. Shannon wasn't looking for an out. She was looking for help and hope to stay in the marriage and encouragement for how she might best influence me. The counselor was biblically correct in providing the "only out" that Jesus mentioned as legitimate grounds for divorce—adultery (although perhaps most Christian counselors now include abandonment and abuse in that category)—but the counselor totally missed Shannon's heart's desire to see our marriage restored.

Shannon discovered that the new church she was attending had a counseling department with trained professional counselors, and their fees were based on the client's ability to pay. Shannon went there for several sessions through March and found their advice much more helpful and biblically sound.

Throughout this period of time, Shannon experienced temptations to have an affair of her own. It was easy to rationalize, "Jimmy was unfaithful to me—and he was a pastor!" She was not looking for a serious relationship, however, but longed for a friend with whom she could talk, go places, and do fun things.

She knew she couldn't stay home all the time, so she began accepting a few dates. One night, after working all week, she decided to go out. "I need to make some friends," she told her parents. Her mom and dad were not interested in going along with her that evening, so Shannon went alone.

She went to a restaurant and sat up at the bar by herself. A man struck up a conversation with her, and they talked easily. Later that week they went on an outing. During their time together, once again, Shannon talked mostly about me. That was the last time she heard from that fellow.

She met another man online and, after a few weeks of interaction on social media, they met in public. "I just need to go and see what happens," Shannon said. Apparently, the experience was disappointing. "He was cute, although not as cute as his online picture. I talked the whole time about Jimmy," Shannon recalls.

"I'd been out of the dating circles for a long time," she said, "and I was surprised how crass the man was to me. He asked if I had any hot, sexy photos I could share with him."

"I just met you!" Shannon told him, shocked at his lack of respect. She walked away with no hesitation.

By early March, Shannon's emotions were frayed, and she couldn't take any more. As she later recalled, "I was in the shower. It had been a particularly sad day, and I'd been listening to a Sara Evans country song, "Stronger," that says, "Even on my weakest days, I get a little bit stronger." I didn't feel that way, but I wanted to. I listened to that song and made it my own, but I had been crying a lot. My thoughts and emotions were running rampant. Again, I thought, 'How could Jimmy leave? We've been together all these years. I don't know anybody here. I'm all alone.'"

"With the warm water streaming over me, I prayed, 'God, I'm done. I can't do this anymore. If You want us together again and want this marriage to work, You are going to have to do it, because I can't.'"

Of course, I knew none of this at the time. I had told Shannon to stop saying she still loved me and to leave me alone. For the most part, she complied. We were polite with each other but were not in any way romantically connected. In one conversation, Shannon had told me during a brief phone conversation that she had gone out with a few other guys, but nothing serious had developed. I was not concerned or swayed by the thought that she might find someone else. If anything, I was indifferent.

Near the end of March, out of the blue, Shannon sent me a platonic text, a nondescript, bland message, just keeping in touch and saying that she missed me. No doubt she was reluctant to say much more since I had been so adamant that I did not want to hear from her.

I did not answer the text from Shannon immediately. Perhaps, because I was still reeling from my recent breakup with Vanessa, I was reticent about responding. Regardless, I waited, then answered Shannon's message later in April. "I'm sorry I can't do the wedding," I wrote to her. "When I think of you, I have good thoughts."

While flying together from Charlotte to San Antonio to attend her brother's wedding, Shannon and her dad had a long conversation. "Shannon, you've got to give it up," he said bluntly. "You and Jim are not getting back together. That's what's wrong with Christians. You think you can just pray and God's going to fix everything."

"Dad, I don't believe that at all," Shannon objected, "but I do believe in prayer and I'm not going to give up. Miracles can happen. You know that I've gone out and tried to meet people. I've tried to get life together and move forward. But I'm not going to stop believing in God or that Jimmy and I might get back together."

"Okay, fine," he huffed.

When the airplane landed, Shannon turned on her phone again, and the text I had sent to her previously popped up.

"Dad, look!" she said. "I got a text from Jimmy."

"What?" He was surprised but reserved. "Okay."

"I'm going to call him and talk to him."

She called me and said, "Why don't you come to San Antonio for the wedding?"

"I can't come," I said. "Not after everything that has happened."

Part of my reticence was because I was embarrassed. And part of my reluctance came from my own experience living in Texas, where a guy could be killed "just because he had it coming to him!" I knew Shannon's family felt awful sadness about how I had hurt her. I wasn't sure I wanted to walk into a situation where I had been the one asked to officiate the marriage ceremony but now could not because I was no longer an ordained minister. Shannon and I talked further, and she again mentioned about me coming to San Antonio for the wedding.

"You need to talk about that with your family first, before we make a decision," I told her.

When she talked with her mom and dad, they grappled with an emotional struggle. Finally, her mom said, "I love Jimmy. Let him come."

Shannon's dad said, "Well, if he is not going to do this anymore, tell him that he is welcome to come visit with his head held high. We won't try to get even with him or to embarrass him for his past actions. And he can come talk with you."

Not every father would respond that way. Most would say, "If you hurt my little girl, you are not going to walk back in here."

I was still reluctant, so I said, "Shannon, I've been working and making good money, but it is all going out to fund the company I started. . . ."

Shannon saw through my smoke screen and my embarrassment. "Do you have something to write with?" she asked.

"Yeah, sure."

"Then take this number down," she said. "This is my credit card number. Put your airline ticket on my credit card."

I could barely believe my ears. This woman was amazing. I had been unfaithful to her, yet she was still willing to give unconditionally to me. I hemmed and hawed for a few more minutes mulling over all the reasons why I couldn't accept her generous offer, but I finally blinked back my objections.

I wrote her credit card number down and purchased a round-trip airline ticket to San Antonio with plans to spend four days there, but not until after the actual wedding that I had been scheduled to perform.

I arrived in San Antonio on Monday after the wedding, and Shannon and her stepdad were at the airport to pick me up. Shannon was hopeful and excited to see me. She walked right up and hugged me.

I hugged her back but much more rigidly. I was still reticent, emotionally guarded, and more reserved than I'd ever been with her. Shannon's parents hugged me as well and did their best to make me feel welcome.

By this time, Vanessa had left me, and Shannon knew that we had broken up, but she didn't know any of the details, especially that Vanessa had been the one to call off the affair, not me.

When I admitted that information to Shannon, she saw it positively. "I don't care how it happened, but I'm glad that it did. At least maybe now we have a chance." Shannon had always taken our wedding vows seriously. For better or for worse—and we had already experienced the worst, so her attitude was "Why not move forward?"

We went out to eat with her mom and stepdad, then went home. Shannon and I shared the same bedroom that night and even the same bed. We were, after all, still married. It felt awkward but good.

Shannon was excited about our potential reconciliation. She just wanted to put the pieces back together, but I was not quite ready for that. My head and heart were not there yet.

I stayed in San Antonio with Shannon from Monday until Friday. We tried to talk in general terms and ascertain whether we could connect again. Many couples who have experienced trouble in their marriages try to focus on "deep talk" without taking the time to build intimate and fun times into their marriage. Serious, difficult discussions about the relationship are usually not the place to start a reconciliation. Shannon and I seemed to sense that, so we avoided digging up the recent past. Instead, we spent time with Shannon's parents and went out to hear some country music.

Shannon was seated in front of me on a bench, listening to the per-
formers. I reached forward and wrapped my arms around Shannon,
and her body melted into mine.

During the time we spent together, we didn't talk about the
heaviest aspects of our situation, such as the affair and how we got
there, much less where we were going from here. I didn't talk about
my vulnerabilities of not feeling accepted or significant. Shannon
didn't talk about her tendency to "go along to get along." Rather
than talking about "our relationship," we spent much more time
engaging in small talk. Besides being far less intimidating, it felt
almost as though we were dating again, talking about insignificant
matters—fun, foolish, even trivial things.

Many couples who are in trouble want to talk about "deep
things," but those sort of heavy-duty relationship discussions are
not fun and frequently fail to build real intimacy. Worse yet, they
often lead to misunderstandings, conflicts, and arguments—the
last things recovering couples need. They'd be much better off
engaging in small talk. We learn much more about each other
in those casual, creative, easygoing conversations than we do in
focused, intense, analysis-type conversations.

Shannon and I kept things simple. We made no firm future
plans; we merely enjoyed being together. I felt as though I knew
what she wanted me to say and do, but I was more cautious than
Shannon, not willing to jump right back into the same scenario
that had led to our separation. No doubt, some of my actions and
responses to her seemed superficial. Nevertheless, we agreed to stay
in touch. I knew that Shannon was praying that we might get back
together, but I couldn't do it because I had not yet figured out why
I had gotten caught up in an affair. Without that answer, I felt sure
I would fall back into familiar patterns.

When we returned to our respective homes on the East Coast,
Shannon began searching online for various marriage counseling

services. She was motivated by the minor victories we had experienced together in San Antonio. She discovered one service that looked promising but was quite expensive, and all the sessions and materials were online.

She continued searching for more personal potential marriage help that she thought might pique my interest, looking in general terms for information on how to save a marriage. She found several intriguing and highly rated services, but one particularly caught her attention. It was called Marriage Helper. Most of the other counseling services were more preventative in nature, but Marriage Helper appeared to deal with couples who were already in deep trouble, with one or both partners having an affair or possibly even having already divorced. Dr. Joe Beam, the founder of Marriage Helper, and his wife, Alice, had divorced and gotten back together after several years apart. Their experience signaled hope to Shannon. "If they can make it, maybe we can do it too."

She had never previously heard of Marriage Helper and really didn't know what to expect from the Save My Marriage Workshop they mentioned in their website materials. But Shannon later said, "My hopes were that Jimmy and I could attend a workshop; maybe he would see me differently, and he would see himself differently. I knew from living with him for twenty years that I couldn't be the one to show him areas where he was wrong. He had to find out for himself." Maybe Marriage Helper really could help. She felt that reaching out was worth a try.

She called the phone number listed on the website and talked to one of Marriage Helper's client representatives.

CHAPTER 27

A Safe Place

One of the more attractive aspects of Marriage Helper to Shannon was talking with a real, live human being rather than simply making choices from an online menu and purchasing seminar or workshop recordings. Shannon explained her situation to the representative, and he listened quietly, asked a few questions, and was quite encouraging. "We see this sort of thing all the time," he said, "dealing with both men and women. We know we can help you."

The representative told Shannon that their primary focus was on doing small group, weekend workshops—usually twenty or thirty couples or so—in various locations around the country. He seemed confident that we would benefit from their program. Shannon gathered the information but made no promises to attend.

When Shannon and I talked next by phone, I could tell immediately that she was excited. "Jimmy, I found a marriage workshop and a place that does counseling that might be able to help us," she gushed.

"I don't need a marriage workshop," I answered her angrily. "I used to *do* marriage counseling. I don't need more of the same.

What are they going to be able to tell me that I don't already know? Why would I want to attend?" I asked. "I was speaking in front of marriage conference crowds while I was having an affair!"

"I don't know," Shannon answered sweetly. "But the fellow who conducts the workshop had an affair, and he and his wife got back together. Maybe they can help us figure some things out."

Despite my skepticism, when I thought more about it, Shannon's suggestion seemed intriguing, but I stubbornly declined nonetheless.

Undeterred, Shannon called back the representative from Marriage Helper and told him my answers. "I'm trying to get Jimmy to come to a workshop, but he says he doesn't need to."

"Well, ask him if I can call him," the rep suggested. "I'll be glad to talk with him. I meet a lot of hardheaded guys, and I think I can answer his concerns."

Shannon forwarded the message on to me, and I reluctantly said, "Yeah, sure, I'll talk to him. But I'm pretty sure it will be a waste of time, both his and mine." I was familiar with numerous well-known marriage counseling organizations, but I had never heard of Marriage Helper.

Sure enough, the Marriage Helper representative called and told me about their program. We had a brief but civil conversation. "No, I don't need that," I told him. "Thanks for calling." I hung up.

But the rep was persistent. Over the next few months, he called back four or five times, not in a pesky sort of way but simply offering to answer any questions or concerns I might have about their workshop. I didn't know squat about their workshop, nor did I care to learn about it, but I attempted to be kind to the man because I assumed that my responses would return to Shannon sooner or later. I was wrong there.

The workshop looked promising, but the closest one in proximity to us was scheduled in July and held in Nashville, on the campus of Lipscomb University. That meant in addition to the expense of the workshop—which was significant—we'd also need money for travel and lodging. Neither Shannon nor I had a great deal of money in savings, and we were both barely eking out a living in our jobs. Moreover, we had not yet sold our home in Massachusetts, so we still had a house payment there plus the insurance, utilities, and maintenance expenses. So when she told me about the workshop, the financial obligation was another reason I was less than enthusiastic about attending.

Shannon's contact from Marriage Helper stayed in touch. The guy was relentless and impossible to throw offtrack; he worked tirelessly to overcome any objections I might come up with. When Shannon indicated that the costs of the workshop and our lack of money were major obstacles to our attending the upcoming weekend event in July, the Marriage Helper representative surprised her. "Maybe we can help," he responded. "We have a few scholarships available that will help pay for the workshop fees and even the lodging. All you have to do is get there."

He gave Shannon several suggestions to pass along to me that might convince me to attend. Shannon knew better. "No, I can't really do that. He won't receive that from me," she told the rep. "I think he needs to hear it from you."

"Okay," the rep replied. "Let me see what I can do." He agreed to call me again, and he did. Slowly but surely, he convinced me that the weekend would be worth it to Shannon and me, whether we got back together or not. "You'll learn more about yourself in one weekend than you ever dreamed possible," he promised. That was a tall order, but it piqued my interest. Maybe I was set on discovering what was wrong with me, or possibly I felt I owed it to Shannon, or perhaps the representative was simply a nice guy, but to my surprise, I heard myself consenting to attend the Marriage Helper workshop. Not that I was greatly enthusiastic or even hopeful about it. I knew all too well that many people attend seminars intending to improve their marriages but walk away more angry than they were previously. Others find genuine hope and help. I had no idea which group Shannon and I might be joining.

Marriage Helper granted a scholarship to both Shannon and me. That meant somebody gave financially who didn't even know our names, and their gift allowed us to attend. Otherwise we may not have been able to afford it. Marriage Helper also arranged for special discounted rates at various hotels nearby the university campus. Shannon searched out the best option and booked it.

Shannon and I had not yet relocated, and both of us were still living with our respective parents. In July I traveled from Virginia to Nashville, and Shannon flew from Charlotte. We arrived and checked in to our hotel, both of us staying in the same room. Although we had stayed together when I had visited her in San Antonio, it still felt awkward to be in a hotel room together after my affair with Vanessa had blown apart our lives. Shannon was gracious, though, and we tried to relax and get some rest before the early morning workshop.

The following morning, we rode to the workshop in my car. On the short drive to the university, I could tell that Shannon was both anxious and excited. She was genuinely hopeful that this could be a significant turning point for us.

I wasn't so sure, but I was trying to be positive in my attitude. After all, it was already a miracle—a number of miracles—that we were even here in this place to attend a marriage workshop! Earlier in the year I had been adamant that I had wanted nothing to do with Shannon. Then, for months, I had flat-out refused to attend a marriage workshop. Yet, against all odds, here we were.

The workshop began promptly on Friday morning at 8:00. Walking in and looking around, I quickly attempted to size up the room and the people in it, recognizing that everyone there was in trouble.

Shannon whispered, "Wow, there are a lot more couples in trouble than I may have thought."

We were both nervous, wondering, *What is going to happen in here?* Anticipation . . . anxiety . . . I don't like someone digging around in my life. We both had been participants in previous marriage seminars, so we wondered, *How is this going to be different?*

But the hosts made us feel comfortable by talking about themselves and some of their marital difficulties. When you know someone else has struggled with the same sort of thing that you have, it gives you some measure of hope.

The seats were at tables arranged in a U-shape so the people attending the workshop could all see each other. Shannon and I sat with a few other couples in the back of the U, on the right-hand side. Looking around, I noticed about twenty people of various ages. All were dressed casually, and most couples sat together, although their body language spoke volumes about the emotional barriers between them. Some seemed perfectly comfortable sitting next to their spouses; others seemed rigid and tense.

Shannon and I were relatively comfortable being together, although both of us were a bit uncertain about what to expect from the workshop. She was more hopeful; I was skeptical. I had attended many marriage-encounter type of events and other marriage improvement seminars. I'd even conducted marriage seminars at our church and had been a guest speaker at others. So I knew the drill—or so I thought.

The hosts opened the workshop by giving us some ground rules. "This is a safe place," the coordinator said. "So we don't want to tear down your spouse. We understand you are hurting, but if you start to speak negatively about your spouse, we will stop you. Remember, this is a safe place."

They also cautioned us about comparing our situation with that of other couples. "During our breaks, please don't go out and talk about details from other people's lives and relationships. That's their story. Stay focused on your story." That wasn't an issue for Shannon and me. We were so focused on ourselves, there wasn't much time to worry about others. But still, it was a good word to all of us about respecting the stories of others.

Although she didn't know everything about what had happened between Vanessa and me, Shannon knew enough that her own heart had been broken. I knew she had every right to reject any possibility of our reconciliation, and I really wasn't seeking it, but the fact that she had fought so hard to get us to the workshop indicated all I needed to know about her willingness to forgive. So all of the workshop rules seemed fair enough to me.

Some people looked miserable, as though they had been dragged to the workshop. We later learned that a few individuals were there simply because their attorney had informed them that if they attended the workshop, then the spouse would sign the divorce papers.

A few others seemed to be playing games. They gave off an air that said, "I'm here, but I'm not really buying into this stuff." Or possibly they, like me, were simply good at pulling off a masquerade.

Regardless, the event facilitators began by helping us better understand our own personalities, how our pasts had influenced us, and what we expected from marriage. The session was relatively lighthearted, considering that the room was filled with failed marriages and hurting people. But the humor helped put us at ease and dispelled a lot of our awkwardness and nervousness. Several couples seemed open to viewing things differently, that the "ropes" that were keeping them together were blessings rather than curses. They expressed hope that they could make changes in their marriages. That encouraged us.

One of the workshop leaders presented a radical idea, but it made a lot of sense to me: "Your old marriage needs to die. This is now a new marriage," the leader said. That we were not simply trying to "get back to normal" was intriguing to me. Indeed, our "normal" had not been working well, so while it may seem to be an admirable goal, to get back to *normal* would have been of little long-term help to us. The idea that we could start again without having to return to a relationship that wasn't working appealed to me.

The most nerve-racking aspects of the first day for Shannon were the sessions in which we split into small groups of married couples and were encouraged to talk about some of our experiences. It was not mandatory that each person share so Shannon didn't say much. More comfortable with speaking in public, I didn't mind talking in front of the group, although it felt strange to share so openly in front of other couples about our relationship and my having an affair. As I looked around at the fourteen faces in our group, I realized that I was not the instructor, trying to teach a lesson; I was not there to encourage anyone. I was talking about me, my mistakes, and my failures. That was a place that, as a leader, I had rarely gone to. And the small group knew that part of the reason I was there had to do with the fact that I was not doing well, that I had screwed up my marriage. Speaking in front of thousands of people had come easily to me. But here, in front of a group of couples who all had banged-up marriages, the sense of exposure and vulnerability and intimacy was awkward for me.

I wasn't telling a "victory" story, talking about how Shannon and I had overcome our problems. I nervously announced that I didn't know squat about our next steps, a statement that didn't surprise anyone in the room.

The counselors handled the sessions skillfully. One woman was especially good. She was kind and quick to encourage the couples to speak openly about their experiences. "Thank you for being willing to share that," she said when someone exposed some vulnerability.

But she was unwilling to placate excuses or rationalizations. "We're sorry you had to go through that," she said whenever anyone tried to make himself or herself sound like a victim. "And we're glad you came here."

But the female facilitator was also firm. "Please don't try to coach others or give advice," she reminded us. "They are in the same situation, so don't take their advice and don't give yours . . . because it is not working for you."

One of the strongest points about the workshop was that it helped us to realize that we were not alone. Other couples that had entered into marriage with the best of intentions now found themselves on the brink of divorce. A few in our group had already been divorced and were hoping to find some means of reconciliation. We realized that we were not "weirdos" or some marital oddity. There were others facing the same sorts of issues Shannon and I were confronting. But although we may be able to commiserate, none of us knew what to do.

The leaders encouraged the workshop participants to ask questions during most of the sessions. That was risky, considering the enormous amount of tension in the room, but when someone's attitude bent toward being belligerent, sarcastically snipping at his or her spouse, or expressing snide innuendo through nonverbal actions or demeanors, the leaders were quick to caution them and calmed things down so everyone could feel as comfortable as possible. Again, we were encouraged to interact with the other couples honestly and openly, without offering advice.

We went to lunch with some of the other workshop attendees, and we all laughed and talked about a few of the things we'd heard that morning. Shannon and I were more upbeat about the workshop than others were, but all seemed hopeful.

The leaders had reminded us that information gathering during the workshop weekend is a process that needs to flow and be connected. "Wait till Sunday and then make your decisions," they said. "Know the facts before you draw any conclusions about your relationship." Of course, we wanted instant answers; most people do, especially when we are hurting. But the workshop leaders advised us to move slowly.

One of the key principles we learned about communication was the need to be a "safe place" to have conversations. The workshop leaders talked about how we build walls in our relationships—some to protect ourselves, some to hide behind. Then, when one or both spouses want to open a conversation, it is like taking down one of the bricks in a wall. "So don't take down a brick and hit your spouse with it!" the leader quipped. "Instead, if you are comfortable with having that conversation, let him or her know that this is a safe place, and it is okay to talk about a particular issue. If it is not comfortable for you, say so before the brick comes down."

This concept piqued my imagination.

Being a safe place for each other facilitated an important piece in our healing—namely, *acceptance.* The workshop leaders emphasized this point: when we stop accepting each other, intimacy dies. On the other hand, acceptance is not tantamount to condoning a person's actions if you feel they are wrong. It is creating a welcoming atmosphere for the *person*, not retaliating or attacking a person for being honest or for admitting his or her failures. Especially when an affair has taken place, the affair is usually a symptom of something broken in the marriage relationship. Certainly, repentance and change are needed, but most people don't wake up some morning and decide to have an affair. It happens over a period of time as wrong choices were made. So to create a safe place where acceptance of the person can occur, even if you hate the events or paths you have taken to get there, is a major first step toward healing a marriage.

Shannon, in particular, found the "safe place" concept helpful, and so did I. Simply knowing that Shannon was committed to being a safe place allowed me to share thoughts, feelings, and emotions with her more readily, some of which were quite painful for both of us to talk about. I tried to be a safe place for her as well. Sometimes in our conversations, Shannon broke down in tears or said, "I need to take a break." But she never attacked me in those conversations. She was safe for me. The "safe place" proved to be a handy communication tool for both Shannon and me that we still use to this day.

The Friday session of the workshop ran till nearly 6:00 p.m. That evening, Shannon and I went out to dinner with another couple attending the workshop and talked in general terms about what we had experienced that day. The husband and wife were subdued in their reactions, but Shannon was genuinely enthusiastic.

After dinner, Shannon and I went back to our hotel room to do our "homework," which was a game assigned by the workshop leaders to help us determine how well we knew each other. "Don't let it become an argument," the leaders cautioned.

Well, that seemed downright silly. We'd been married for twenty years! How well do you really know your spouse? Nevertheless, Shannon and I played the game. It was fun but also eye-opening as we realized how much we really *didn't* know about each other after twenty years of marriage.

We felt good about what we were learning. But there were a lot of emotions going on in both of us—we were confident, scared, sad, nervous, all at the same time. Hearing how our behaviors had hurt each other saddened both Shannon and me. We tried to avoid statements such as, "Yeah, I hurt you, but here's what you did to me." As our workshop leaders reminded us, "*But* is a big word. In an apology, that one word often negates everything else you said before that. It is saying, 'Everything that I've said prior to this doesn't matter. This wasn't my fault.' It is almost always heard by the other person as a challenge or an excuse or a rationalization." So we did our best to avoid those kinds of words.

Our instructors suggested, "Rather than using *but*, it is often better to simply say, 'I'm sorry.' Then come back later and acknowledge the situation with a statement such as, 'When you do this, it has this influence on me.' Allowing a bit of time before broaching the subject may help defuse the tension. To plunge into the discussion in the heat of the moment is often seen as defensive and causes your partner to feel, 'He (or she) is not hearing me.'"

Shannon acknowledged that deep inside, she had already determined that she wanted our marriage to work. She believed that even after prolonged lapses of love, it was possible to rebuild.

I was hopeful, but I wasn't there yet.

CHAPTER 28

GAME CHANGER

Back in the classroom on Saturday morning, most couples seemed more comfortable facing the second day of the workshop, but some seemed even more stressed and agitated than they had the previous day. I was comfortable and interested, fascinated by the practical approach and the statistical information the workshop leaders presented.

But then about midday, when Dr. Joe Beam, founder of Marriage Helper, told his personal story, I sat mesmerized. It was as though he was talking about me, my feelings, my insecurities, and offering insights that, for the first time, helped me understand how and why I could have gotten caught up in an affair.

Joe talked about limerence, a new term to me, even though I had studied psychology and had counseled numerous people embroiled in troubled marriages, with one or both members of the couple involved in sexual affairs. Limerence, Joe explained, was when a person becomes romantically infatuated with another, mentally and emotionally dwelling on him or her almost constantly in hopes of having those feelings reciprocated. A person in limerence might possibly become so obsessed with that other person that the relationship seems close to love, but it is quite destructive. Often, a person caught up in a limerence type of affair sees only the attractive qualities in the object of his or her desires and does not see the other person's faults, although they are easily seen by others. So even though you may be fantasizing about or even having sex with someone outside your marriage, you are not building true intimacy with that person. Most limerence relationships, Joe suggested, last between three months and three years, but rarely longer.

Joe was a fountain of practical wisdom, reminding us of things that simply made sense. One statement he made especially connected in my mind. "People will not leave what they have unless they believe what they are going to is better." But sometimes, if someone believes it so badly, they will go to nothing. They figure it is better to be alone than to endure what they are experiencing.

As Joe talked about his own vulnerabilities, it sounded as though he was listing my own. He emphasized that feeling insignificant and invisible made someone like me extremely susceptible to attention.

Moreover, like Joe had done with his wife, Alice, I had villainized Shannon, saying derogatory things about her to other people. Most of those people looked back at me as if to say, "Are you nuts? You're out of your mind! Shannon is a godsend! She is a wonderful person." Nevertheless, I attempted to "rewrite" history, saying such things as, "I never really loved Shannon; I was never crazy about her." In truth, I had adored her.

Other people—and even the church—that might have been barriers to me moving into an affair suddenly became enemies to me, at least in my own mind. Similarly, I lived in a fantasy state of my own, thinking about Vanessa and texting her repeatedly.

All of these things, Joe explained, were significant indicators of limerence.

I had not previously thought about that, but I now realized that what I didn't know could indeed hurt both Shannon and me. In fact, one of the worries that prevented me from plunging full force into reconciliation with Shannon was the fear that I might repeat my immoral, duplicitous actions. I had cheated on her with one woman. What was to keep me from doing it again, especially if nothing had changed for me?

But as Joe analyzed the anatomy of an affair and explained how limerence lures a person into one, I realized that it was not some undisclosed evil that I could not identify and whose power I was under. Instead, I had made a series of poor choices, most of which stemmed from my own insecurities and insufficiencies. Joe also talked about the physiological aspects of an affair and how the rises of dopamine or deficiencies of serotonin in a person's system influence the decision-making process. In limerence, rises in dopamine produce feelings of ecstasy ("I can do anything! I'm excited; it feels good"), while serotonin, a self-control drug that normally enhances calm feelings, decreases. Happening together, these chemical changes in a person's brain can produce a poor environment for wise decision-making.

At the same time, passion is intensified by fear, Joe explained. It could be fear of getting caught or fear of losing the other person. Regardless, the fear will make an affair more attractive. "I'm afraid that I am not going to have time for a shared experience with you, that I might lose you, so we have to take advantage of this opportunity. I need to be with you more! It is you and me against the world, so we have to stay close to each other."

Joe described how the faithful spouse often becomes the enemy because the unfaithful, infatuated partner looks at that person as coming between his or her limerence person that he or she wants to be with. This can result in unexplainable, uncharacteristic meanness. At several points during Dr. Beam's talk, Shannon looked at me as if to say, "Yep, that's you!"

What Joe described resonated with me. So much so that in the middle of the session, I leaned over to Shannon and whispered to her. "I know what happened now," I said. "We can do this. Now I know that we can get back together."

Shannon looked back at me, her eyes wide in amazement and excitement.

"Shhh," I said, "we'll talk about it later." Shannon nodded and her countenance brightened.

This workshop session was a game changer for me.

Suddenly, I had hope. For the first time, I felt as though I could understand why I had been unfaithful to the woman I truly loved.

In one hour, Joe shed more light into my heart and mind than I had experienced in twenty years of marriage and ministry. Now that I knew why I had engaged in an affair, I could also find ways to avoid it and hopefully compensate for my own inadequacies.

Significantly, Shannon, too, realized for the first time that she had been contributing to my sense of insignificance. She had never before heard of limerence prior to the workshop's Saturday session, but now she realized why even some of her kind, loving expressions over the past twenty years were slowly pushing me away.

We recalled, for instance, an occasion in which I had asked her to get something I needed for a meeting from our parked car at the church in Connecticut. On the way to get the item, Shannon encountered a pastor friend of ours who said, "Aw, he doesn't need that." Shannon returned without the item I had requested, and then, as it turned out, I did indeed need the item. I was furious. "You listened to him?" I asked. It bugged me that she had chosen to ignore what I wanted, what I had specifically asked for, and instead did what she felt was right. It seemed as if she was more worried about what the pastor might think, so she wanted his approval. More importantly, we now realized, I was upset because her actions contributed to me feeling unimportant and insignificant. Shannon was just making sure and doing due diligence by covering her bases. But to me it was an indication of disrespect. Whether it was or not was irrelevant, but that's how I perceived it. We began to consider how we could handle similar situations in better ways.

As we had the day before, we also had sessions on Saturday where we split into smaller groups. The leaders wanted us to discuss some of the things we had heard in the workshop and how they related to our lives. In one such group, Joe Beam guided our discussions and, almost against my will, I found myself participating fully, talking frequently, and sharing my experiences and feelings. Dr. Beam didn't say anything to me at the time, but I could tell by the way he kept his gaze on mine that he had been listening carefully to what I was saying.

We were even more hopeful after the Saturday workshop sessions ended. Later that night, when Shannon and I returned to our room after dinner, I could tell she was pondering something. Dr. Beam had taught us to use the two-question principle when approaching tough subjects in our conversations about our marriage: one, "Are you sure you want to know this?" and two, "Can you be a safe place?" These two questions helped get us into the right mindset to be successful in discussing difficult subjects, so Shannon started there.

"Can I ask you a question?" she finally said. As she had learned at the workshop, Shannon emphasized that it was a "safe place" to talk about some delicate matters.

"When did the affair with Vanessa begin?" she asked.

"Are you sure you want to know this?" I asked, just as Joe had advised us.

"Yes, I do."

Although the early stages of the affair seemed like a blur, I told Shannon as much as I could remember.

On Sunday morning, the last day of the workshop, the facilitators talked about forgiveness as well as setting goals together, aspirations, and learning how to be together. They also gave us some guidelines to help in reconciliation. "While you are here, you have all of us to help you," they said, "but when you leave here, you have to remind yourself about some of the keys to better relationships that you have discovered."

The workshop concluded late Sunday afternoon, and most couples who had attended, including Shannon and me, seemed inspired and encouraged. Although I had participated in and even conducted numerous marriage seminars, I had never experienced anything quite like this workshop.

After the final session, as everyone was leaving, I saw Dr. Beam sitting in the back of the classroom. He looked tired and wrung out from speaking and directing the entire weekend event.

"Doctor Beam, I want to thank you for this weekend," I said as I shook his hand. "It has been really helpful and encouraging."

We talked a bit, and Joe said, "Well, son, you're a pretty good speaker." Joe had heard me talking in our breakout groups, and he could tell that I was comfortable talking in front of a group of people.

"Thank you, sir," I said. "I was a minister and I used to speak in public a lot." We chatted further before Shannon and I said goodbye to Joe. "We're ready to go, but I want to thank you because this has made a big difference in our relationship."

Dr. Beam thanked me, but before he said goodbye, he looked at me and said, "Son, can I ask you a question?"

"Of course."

"If or when the time comes, and you feel good, do you think you'd like to do this? I think you'd be pretty good at rescuing marriages."

Say what? I could hardly believe my ears. This man didn't know me.

"Well, thank you very much. But I'm not really interested in working with people," I said. My faith in God and His people was still fractured and feeble.

Joe smiled. "It wasn't a job offer," he quipped. "It is just something for you to think about."

"Thank you, sir," I answered with a laugh.

To my total surprise, I left the workshop encouraged and inspired. Even more than our marriage issues, I had learned more about myself just as the workshop representative had predicted. Shannon was especially excited because I had told her, "We can do this."

On the other hand, despite our newfound hope, Shannon and I both had to return to our separate locations, Shannon to South Carolina and me to Virginia. When Shannon had moved to South Carolina in February, she had made a commitment to her employer to remain there until the end of the year. As we walked through the airport toward our respective flights, we agreed, "We'll talk soon about all this." We hugged and kissed goodbye, then embarked to our separate destinations. But we left carrying something we hadn't come with—hope.

At that point, Marriage Helper did not have a great deal of follow-up materials other than the workshop workbook; Joe's book, *The Art of Falling in Love*; and John Gottman's *Seven Principles for Making Marriage Work*.

We were pretty much on our own to apply what we had learned. Over the next few weeks, Shannon and I talked frequently by telephone, usually every other night, attempting to revisit some of the concepts we had learned at the workshop. When possible, either Shannon or I would travel to visit. As much as we enjoyed the visits, they were not marvelous romantic interludes. We still hadn't sold our home in Massachusetts, so we also had to deal with real life issues such as paying the mortgage, managing the bills, and attempting to enhance the home for quicker sale, all while trying to produce new sources of income.

We didn't even consider moving back there, although in some ways that may have made sense financially. But there were too many memories there, too many people who knew us and who knew about what had happened. If we had any hope at all of surviving the mess I had made, we knew we needed a fresh start somewhere else.

Shannon's parents were cautiously optimistic. They were happy that Shannon's spirits had perked up, but they did not want her to naively move back in with me. "Make sure he isn't going to do it again," they said every way they could. They encouraged me not to rush but to take things slowly.

They understood that we were still married, but they had hardly interacted with me over the past two years, so they couldn't really tell if I was being authentic with Shannon or not. Sometimes I wondered myself.

CHAPTER 29

REBUILDING TRUST

Coming out of the workshop, Shannon and I still weren't "fixed." We now had to apply the things we had learned and continue to dismantle the walls of separation that we had built over the years. That was a process, and as much as we desired instantaneous results, both Shannon and I knew that the transformation was going to take some time. Like most couples, we experienced occasions when we knew what to do but chose the opposite or wrong decisions. When we made those kinds of mistakes, we had to face up to them honestly, admit our failures, and find better ways of dealing with issues.

For instance, Shannon memorized the words of 1 Corinthians 13, the well-known "love chapter" in the Bible. Love is kind . . . true love endures all things; love doesn't count offenses . . . doesn't keep score; true love never fails.

We both believed that the Bible gives the greatest example of what true love is all about.

Nevertheless, Shannon struggled with the practical application of love when it came to forgiveness. She sometimes brought up the past; she had forgiven me, but she couldn't merely act as if the past had not happened. She knew what had happened all too well. She forgave, but she did not have to accept what I had done. She wanted our relationship to continue on the basis of honesty, so we had to sit down and discuss what that meant—for both of us.

Though we now had the tools for improving our marriage, we still had a lot of work to do, especially in what it meant to affirm and be honest with each other. We recognized that we both had to adjust to a new way of regarding the other's behavioral style and interacting with each other. We weren't enemies; we loved each other, but our perceptions and expectations of how that love operated were different.

Because our personality traits are so different, it was sometimes awkward for me to express my genuine need and not to mention feelings of being slighted. I understood that Shannon wanted to please me. She had always tried to please me from the beginning of our marriage. But what she thought I needed, and what I felt that involved, were often two different things. Shannon recalls, "I was always uplifting Jimmy and telling him how amazing he is. But that's not what he needed. He needed me to help him when he felt insignificant."

At the risk of seeming like a selfish ogre, I had to find a way to let Shannon know that it mattered to me whether she remembered to purchase the Necco wafers and grapes at the grocery store. I grappled with how to convey to her the importance of those little things without seeming overbearing. To me, it wasn't about the candy or the fruit; it was about how I felt whenever she forgot or ignored my requests. It was as though she was saying, "Your desires don't matter to me. *You* don't matter, and I don't love you enough to care about what matters to you." She wasn't actually saying that, but remember: perception matters.

Of course, I was grateful for her desires to please me, even if she didn't always hit the bull's-eye. I appreciated that she *wanted* to please me and was trying.

For her part, Shannon avoided conflict or sharing her own opinions or desires. Even if pressed against her will, her attitude was "I need to take one for the team."

For instance, earlier in our marriage, I might say to her, "I'm in the mood for some Mexican food. What would you like?"

She would answer, "Oh, I don't care. Mexican is fine," even if she preferred to have Italian food that night.

That led to problems later because, eventually, I simply stopped asking. But in a relationship, both partners need a voice and both need to be heard. So we worked hard at Shannon's speaking up regarding what she truly wanted and my listening in a manner that did not intimidate her. I practiced keeping my body language open, avoided crossing my arms over my chest during our conversations, and tried to control my loud vocal responses or stern facial expressions.

I struggled to find a balance between being Shannon's protector and provider while not treating her as a child who could not make up her mind or make serious decisions on her own. Again, that wasn't as easy as it might seem since Shannon's personality lent itself to being more passive. I knew that Shannon actively avoided conflict. So I encouraged her, "Tell me what you like. Tell me what you want. Don't let me roll over you and make the decisions. Say what you want." Sometimes I gently forced her to make a decision, even if it was as minor as picking where we ate dinner that evening.

I also had to learn how to speak so she could tell me in a safe way what she truly liked or did not. I couldn't assume that I knew what Shannon wanted, nor could she anticipate my responses.

To this day, I'm still quite susceptible to feelings of insignificance, and sometimes even the tiniest event can set me back. For instance, my real mom and my stepdad, Stan, came to visit Shannon and me in Virginia after we had built a new house there.

I wanted to show Mom a good time, and I enjoy cooking, so I normally made breakfast and dinner every day during their stay.

One morning I set about preparing breakfast for everyone, assuming I'd fry some bacon and eggs and make some pumpkin pancakes from scratch. To figure out how much I needed of the various ingredients, I wanted to get a ballpark figure of how many people wanted to eat pancakes. So I took a poll of the family. "Shannon, would you like some pumpkin pancakes?"

"Oh, yes. Thank you!"

"Stan, would you like some pumpkin pancakes?"

"That would be great."

"Mom, would you like to have some pumpkin pancakes?"

"No, I don't like pumpkin pancakes," she responded.

"Okay, no problem, I'll have some other things for you to eat," I assured her. I made enough pancake mix for Shannon, Stan, and me and then fried up the bacon and eggs, waiting to make the pancakes last so they wouldn't get cold.

After serving up some great-looking pancakes for Shannon and Stan, I got down to the last portions of pancake mix. I plopped a couple of dollops into the pan for my own pancakes and watched them rise, my mouth watering to the point of almost drooling the whole time. Suddenly, Mom came around the corner, stuck her nose in the air, and said, "Hey, Jim, those smell pretty good. I think I'll try a couple of those pumpkin pancakes."

"But I only made enough . . ." I began and then stopped. The significance of her statement hit me like a two-by-four whacking me between the eyes. Instantly it triggered a switch inside me. My mind went back to my childhood when, as I now believed, Mom's decisions had cost other people dearly, including me. Yet she seemed oblivious to the impact her choices made on others and appeared to have no consideration for the feelings of loss those around her experienced. As a youngster, I felt that I had to make up for Mom's decisions. She'd screw things up, and I'd have to adjust my life accordingly, hoping to "fix it." I never could.

"Okay, fine," I said curtly. I gave Mom my pancakes. As I did, I thought, *She is still doing this to me. I am so insignificant to her that she can change her mind on a whim, regardless of how it affects me, as long as it makes her feel better.*

That attitude had tainted my life from the time I was a child. Consequently, I allowed few people to get close to me.

I knew it wasn't about pancakes. It was about all those years of me feeling insignificant because of the actions or attitudes of someone else.

In a similar way, for most of my early life, I'd felt that my brother, Marcus, had a relationship with our father that I never got to have. Dad was there for my brother, supporting him in ways he did not always demonstrate to me, and as a result, I was jealous of my brother. I had hoped my entire life to impress our dad that I could be good at something. Meanwhile, Marcus didn't even seem to notice the dichotomy. He simply assumed Dad's acceptance and approval and took it for granted, but I was not that secure. *Why am I not worthy of Dad's attention?* I wondered.

For the longest time, I thought that was the reason I felt hurt and jealous. But it wasn't. I realized for the first time that my bitterness and frustration was not because I could never impress my dad or that I was jealous of my brother. My greatest hurt stemmed from my own sense of insignificance.

I now know that much of this contradiction was due to my own perception. But it wasn't until years later that I learned about "expectation bias," that an individual's expectations about a particular outcome greatly influence that person's perceptions of *someone else's* behavior. For instance, when I observed Marcus and Dad's relationship, if I perceived that Dad always loved him the most, I regarded everything that Marcus said or did, or that my parents did for him, through my preconceived notions.

Even though I was wrong, my own happiness and connection to my parents became a competition with my brother—one that sometimes created conflict between Marcus and me because of my own insecurities. It wasn't his fault; it was mine. How silly. How unnecessary and damaging such perceptions can be.

Moreover, I realized that I had carried these same sort of biased expectations into my relationship with Shannon. For instance, when Shannon interrupted me in a conversation, it played right into my negative feelings, even though she had no intention of doing something detrimental or offensive. But to me, her interruptions trumpeted the message, "If I were important, you would not interrupt me. So I must not be significant."

"See, you always interrupt me, Shannon," I said—which, of course, was not true, but it was my perception.

"Okay," she said, "I was just trying to ask you some questions to improve our communication, but I understand that I tend to interrupt you, so I will work on trying not to do that." And she did, but because of my own expectation bias, I did not even notice. My prejudices were still deeply embedded in my mind. I didn't recognize that Shannon had stopped interrupting me; I simply assumed that she always would, so that's what I expected.

Not long after that, Shannon and I were engaged in a serious conversation, and I noticed that she was raising her eyebrows frequently but not saying much. After a while I said, "What are you doing? Aren't you going to say anything?"

"I'm listening," she said. "I'm trying not to interrupt you." We both broke out laughing as we realized that we were making progress in our communication. But I had to recognize the issue of my own bias—assuming that she was interrupting me because I was insignificant—before we could change our behavior.

For most people, the hot-button issue would not be interruptions, Necco wafers, grapes, or pancakes. It might be a wife's failure to replace her husband's screwdriver or wrench after using it; it may be the husband's laziness in not putting his clothes in the hamper; it might be the wife's tendency to leave dirty coffee cups in the couple's car. Perhaps it is leaving lights on, or setting the heat or air-conditioning to excessive temperatures in disregard of your partner's preferences. It could be a person's obsession with fiddling around on a smartphone while ignoring the presence of his or her spouse. Counselors used to joke about married couples who fought over whether the toothpaste should be squeezed from the bottom of the tube or the middle or whether the toilet paper should roll from the top or bottom of the roll. Those issues aren't so funny for many couples. While these minor offenses may seem insignificant to one person, to another they are flagrant indications that his or her spouse really does not care what the other person thinks, prefers, needs, or desires. Experience enough of that sort of thing and the message comes across loudly: "You don't really love me." That produces a seething volcano of emotions, ready to erupt at the slightest increase in pressure or provocation.

That was what Shannon and I were forced to grapple with when we began putting our marriage back together. Basically, after twenty years of marriage, we were trying to learn each other's needs. We had to relearn that simple principle: "It's not all about me." It's not all about me in the sense that our past failures are not all my fault, nor is it about me getting my needs met. It is about both spouses' deepest needs being regarded with sensitivity, caring, respect, and love.

In better times, Shannon had occasionally said to me, "If you cheat on me, you're gone."

I often responded to her, "Well, if that is the case, you must not really love me. If you really love unconditionally, if he or she does something bad, you would forgive and give that person another chance."

Shannon wasn't buying it. "No," she said, "it is a character issue. If you really love, you won't cheat." We chuckled over our rigid positions. That was fine when we were talking about theories, but when it actually happened, when I actually had an affair, and when Shannon faced the temptation of having an affair, we both had to decide how we were going to move forward. Shannon decided that forgiveness was the better option. "God is a forgiving God, so I wanted to forgive Jimmy too. Why would I want to give up what we have?" Shannon said later. "I've met so many people who have gotten divorced because they found someone else who met the needs in which they were deficient or that their spouse wasn't meeting. But then, soon after, they realized they were better matched with their original partner. With Jimmy, I at least knew what I had. Sure, we needed to work on our marriage, but we had a lot of good things going for us."

Shannon continued, "Some friends asked, 'Why didn't you divorce and move on?' I felt certain that the person saying and doing those awful things to me was not the Jimmy I knew. The Jimmy I knew wasn't there. I believed that Jimmy was a good person who did a bad thing—and that's different than a bad guy doing bad things—so I felt like I needed to find that good guy again.

"In some ways, it might have been easy to divorce and remarry," Shannon admitted. "But let's be honest: first, I'd have to find someone compatible with whom I wanted to commit my life. Then, too often, we discover that the grass really isn't greener on the other side of the fence. I felt that if I divorced Jimmy, I'd probably be looking for someone like him. I already know what I'm dealing with now. Why not try to make our relationship better rather than going after a redo?"

As difficult as it was, we learned that we could not always let our feelings be our guides. As Shannon put it, "Feelings are real, but they are not always true." How we interpret what transpired influences our feelings. Now Shannon will say, "I don't like the way you spoke to me because it makes me feel foolish."

It would do little good—and I really didn't have the right—to say, "Well, you shouldn't feel that way." Whether I think she should or shouldn't feel a certain way is irrelevant. She *does* feel that way. So we started from there and moved forward.

Sometimes, even when the information is not factually correct, the resultant feelings are real. Imagine, for instance, that a state trooper shows up at our home and says, "Mr. Pourteau, there's been a horrible accident. We have found your automobile and your wife's purse inside. We also found Ms. Pourteau's driver's license. I'm sorry to tell you that the curly-haired woman driving the car did not make it. I'm afraid that your wife has perished in that accident."

Hearing that news, I would be devastated.

But then, forty-five minutes later, another police officer knocks on my door. "Mr. Pourteau, we are so sorry. We made a mistake. We have located Ms. Pourteau. Your wife had allowed her friend to borrow her car and had left her purse in the car when she went in to have her nails done. The person we extricated from the vehicle was not your wife."

How would I feel? I would be ecstatic that my wife was safe, even though I would be sad that her friend had died.

So the question is, Which feelings were wrong?

Neither. The feelings were real in both cases. For most people, perception is reality. Whether something is true or not often doesn't matter. What matters is the perception of what is true to that person.

We tend to tell people not to judge or not to feel a certain way whenever we are expressing conflicting emotions. "You shouldn't feel that way," we may protest.

"But I do feel that way!"

Regardless whether the facts of a situation were correct, Shannon and I discovered that the feelings are real, so we attempt to be more sensitive to each other, whether or not we both agree or feel the same way.

We now operate more carefully when it comes to "taking bricks down" from the walls we built to protect ourselves. We have learned to ask, "Are you sure you want to know this?" and "Are you a safe place right now?" If the answer is yes, to Shannon, that means, "Jimmy is going to tell me something right now, and I do not want to attack him." Sometimes the answer is no, and that is okay. Perhaps Shannon decides that she really doesn't need to know an answer. Or maybe we are tired, hungry, or in a bad mood. That isn't the best time for difficult discussions. "Give me a little time," Shannon says on occasion. If we tell each other something and the other person isn't "safe," before long the communication will break down or possibly stop altogether. When we choose to take a brick down, we have to feel safe in doing so or else we will add more bricks to the wall, making it even higher.

The Marriage Helper workshop and the mentorship of Dr. Joe Beam facilitated our getting back on the love path and doing the things that caused us to fall in love in the first place. It reminded us that we needed to be the best version of ourselves that we could possibly be—physically, intellectually, emotionally, and spiritually.

We also worked a great deal on practical ways of rebuilding trust in our relationship. Like Humpty Dumpty, broken trust is not easily pieced back together again. But we knew we had to start somewhere. Shannon boldly asked me questions, and I was always willing to answer as truthfully and as honestly as I could—but always with one caveat.

"Just be sure: do you really want the answer?" I said. The workshop leaders had used the illustration of toothpaste: once it is out of the tube, it is hard to put it back inside. Our words are similar. Even if we say, "I take it back," once those words have been spoken, they have an indelible life of their own. So when Shannon asked those delicate questions, I did my best to make sure that she truly wanted the truth before I spouted some knee-jerk response.

At the same time, Shannon committed to being a safe place. She fought hard with herself to make sure that she "took down a brick" anytime she questioned me or we entered a delicate discussion. She adopted a position similar to President Ronald Reagan's famous adage regarding the Russians and their nuclear program: "Trust but verify." Sometimes Shannon asked me a question, then followed up with the same question a few days later, just to see if I changed my answer.

Usually I did not, but if I fudged a little, I encouraged Shannon to challenge me, and she would—even though it went against her natural personality traits.

To further engender my wife's trust in me, I gave Shannon unfiltered, complete access to my phone and computer, providing her with all the passwords so she could enter any of my accounts at any time to view my activities. I wasn't trying to circumvent her knowledge in any way, so I willingly offered to provide as much "security" as I could, hoping to incrementally rebuild her trust in me.

If I went out someplace with a friend, I often called Shannon from the location, sometimes sending a photo on my phone so she could see that I was, in fact, where I said I was. "I'm really here," I sometimes quipped. Of course, we both knew that any phone applications could be beaten by a technologically savvy person if someone really wanted to do so. I didn't. I wanted to rebuild Shannon's trust in me, so I tried to keep her informed regarding my whereabouts and my estimated time of arrival back home.

We knew we could do those things only so long before they became irritations. More importantly, we wanted to extend trust as fully as possible. We didn't want external, superficial controls constraining us. We wanted to build trust in each other, not in artificial fences we constructed around our emotions or actions. Eventually, Shannon said, "I can't live like this. I don't want you to feel that I am constantly checking up on you. I just need to trust you." She didn't want to monitor my activities to gauge my love for her. Nor did I have any desire to keep tabs on my wife. We chose to trust each other.

That was refreshing to me since I felt as though I had been walking on eggshells, gingerly trying not to make a mistake.

At times Shannon asked me hard questions. I didn't mind her probes, but sometimes she posed "what if?" questions. That was always counterproductive. "What if Vanessa had not called off the affair? What if we had remained in Connecticut instead of moving? What if Vanessa had gotten pregnant?" Those questions were always stumbling blocks for me (I had no idea how to answer her hypothetical queries) and unhealthy gristle for Shannon. The "what ifs" were an assault on reality and an attack on her happiness. So she found it better to simply ask me point-blank when she had specific questions to which she needed to know the answers. More often than not, when I asked Shannon if she really wanted to know, after some consideration, she frequently said, "No, I really don't. I don't need those images."

At the same time, she meticulously guarded her heart and mind. During that time she refused to watch Hallmark movies or other television shows that presented marriage as the idyllic life of perpetual romantic bliss, or the opposite, that someone was always cheating on his or her marriage partner. Such input could cause her to doubt my sincerity. As much as she loved country music, she discovered that she couldn't listen to "cheatin' songs." She avoided other country music songs that she really enjoyed because they evoked such strong memories in her mind. When one of those triggers fired, Shannon changed the tune or the channel so she wouldn't dwell on negative images.

But she didn't merely rid her mind of the negative images. She replaced those images with positive ideas on which she wanted to focus. Shannon understood that our minds have difficulty processing negative things and that we can't merely "not think about it." Those negative thoughts, attitudes, and actions must be replaced with something positive. That wasn't as hard as it might seem. For instance, she not only avoided reading romance novels but started reading her Bible more frequently along with other books offering inspiration and hope.

• • • • •

It was January 2012 before Shannon and I finally moved into the same house together in Prince George, Virginia, on a permanent basis. Marcus and I had hoped to take over our dad's construction company since he was retiring, so Shannon and I moved to my parents' home with Marcus after my parents moved out. Before long, Marcus invited his fiancée to move in, and that created another awkward situation.

Shannon and I were just getting back together, battling for the survival of our marriage, which would have been difficult enough, but now we were living with my brother and his girlfriend. Shannon did not know Marcus's fiancée at all, and due to our personalities, Marcus and I occasionally rubbed each other the wrong way.

Don't get me wrong: I loved my brother, and we had a lot of fun together, even living in such close quarters. I often joked that I wished I were him. He was handsome and possessed movie-star good looks; he was instantly popular with everyone who met him.

In times of need, my brother and I have always been there for each other. I could easily recall just a year earlier, when I moved back in with my parents. I barely had any money in my pocket and certainly had nothing in savings. I was flat broke and wondering what I was going to do. How was I going to survive?

My brother walked into the house one day and found me in tears. "Jim, what's up? What's the matter?" Marcus asked with genuine concern in his voice.

"I don't know," I said. "My life is a mess, and I'm embarrassed. I can't believe where I am. Look at me. I've got nothing and I don't know which way to turn."

Marcus left the room and came back a few minutes later. He handed me a stack of money and said, "Here, take this. And don't worry about paying me back. There's no need. It's a gift."

"No, no, I can't do that," I said.

"Why not? You'd do the same for me." He was right. When I counted the money, it was more than two thousand dollars, and I desperately needed it.

Sometimes angels look a lot like your brother.

Marcus and I loved each other, but living together as four adults in a small house with my spouse and his future wife—along with three dogs and a cat—was just a zoo! More importantly, Shannon and I needed to work on "us," and the cramped conditions created extra tension that none of us needed.

It was a challenging time. We had no furniture of our own, and Shannon was working from home. Before long, Shannon wisely observed, "Jimmy, we need to get our own space."

I agreed, and we moved to a luxury condominium in Petersburg. Ironically, we weren't there long before Marcus got married and he and his bride, Adrienne, moved into the same complex.

That was okay with us. It was fun having them living near us—even better now that we were no longer sharing bathrooms!

CHAPTER 30

HOODWINKED OR
GOD-SMACKED?

Nine months later, I was reminiscing about my conversation with Dr. Joe Beam following the workshop. I felt sure that he had been sincere when he suggested that at some point in the future I might be valuable to his organization. I called Dr. Beam and asked, "What do we need to do to make this happen?"

"Come spend some time with us," Joe suggested.

I began accompanying Joe to workshops, learning the material, and observing how he worked with couples who were in deep trouble in their marriages. Since I was not actively participating in the workshop, it was easy for me to notice how Joe's approach differed from other marriage seminars. It was also different from my own experience in speaking at marriage conferences prior to having the affair. Joe's material was much more research-based than that of other marriage workshops. His was not merely rosy, "pie in the sky" encouragement; he provided specific answers and positive next steps in rebuilding a marriage. Couples seemed to respond to his more educational approach merged with practical applications of the material, things they could actually incorporate into their marriages.

On one occasion, Joe invited me to join him for a "Love, Sex, and Marriage" event that he was conducting for about one thousand attendees at a church in Mission, Texas, right near the US-Mexico border. I absorbed Joe's teaching like a sponge and took copious notes. At one point during the conference, Joe was speaking on the platform, describing a person he knew who modeled integrity, talent, wisdom, and authenticity, when out of the blue he suddenly said, "My buddy, Jimmy, is here today. Come on up here, Jimmy!"

I was shocked. First, Joe described me in such glowing terms that it was nearly overwhelming. But then he wanted me to join him on stage, which surprised me even further. *What is he up to?* I wondered, but there was no time to consider the options. Joe was waiting and more than a thousand people were watching with intense curiosity.

I slowly walked up onto the platform and looked out into a group of faces wearing expressions similar to ones Shannon and I had during our first workshop barely a year ago. I stood next to Joe, who was smiling broadly. I had no warning of what he was about to do. Joe looked at me with a twinkle in his eyes and said, "Why don't you tell the folks what God has done with you and Shannon."

I could hardly believe my ears. *Joe! Are you out of your mind? You know I've felt disqualified from ever standing up and speaking again.* Joe and I had discussed that some of my friends had drilled into my head and heart that if a pastor commits a moral failure such as sex outside of marriage, he is excluded from ministry for the rest of his life; he is done. There is no place for that person in the ministry. Of course, I knew that Joe did not harbor similar notions of ministerial disqualification, but he was aware of how profoundly those kinds of statements had impacted me. I didn't mention that to Joe while standing next to him on stage because I respected him so much. If Joe asked me to do something, I'd try.

But I was nervous. It was the first time I had been on a stage since I resigned from the church. I had no prepared talk or notes to go by. Why would I? I'd had no idea that Joe was going to put me on the spot like this! It was also a bit risky for Joe since he had little idea what I might say. I tried to compose my thoughts and emotions, beginning slowly but speaking straightforwardly and honestly about my relationship with Shannon. I took the next five to ten minutes to tell an abbreviated version of our story.

Once I conquered my initial jitters, the words flowed easily—almost too easily—as I relaxed on stage, back in my element again. I finished up on a hopeful note, and the workshop group seemed to appreciate my honesty and transparency in telling them our journey. They applauded enthusiastically.

Why are they clapping? I wondered. *I had an affair and nearly destroyed our marriage.* Then it hit me. In telling our story and admitting how awful I had been to Shannon, I had lent the audience some hope: if God could restore our marriage, something similar could happen to theirs.

Afterward, Joe was encouraging. "I knew you could do it," he said with a smile. "You *needed* to do it. You needed to get back in the saddle. Whether or not you ever preach again, you need to get back to being the person God designed you to be."

Although I would have declined to speak had Joe asked me earlier, the way that he did it sort of hoodwinked me into getting back on the platform. And I was grateful.

"Thank you, Joe," I said. "You tricked me, but I do appreciate your confidence in me." Looking back, I can now see the wisdom in what Joe did. That day was a turning point for me.

When I called Shannon later that day, I huffed, "You're not going to believe this. Joe put me on stage!" I expected Shannon to commiserate with me and tell me how unfair it was for Joe to surprise me like that.

She did nothing of the sort. "Good!" she gushed. "That's great!" I realized that Shannon believed in me and was still my best cheerleader. I sat back and cried. *How could she possibly feel this way after all I had done?*

Only the mercy and grace of God could explain it: because of His mercy, He didn't give me what I deserved, and because of His grace—His unmerited, unearned favor—He gave me far more than I deserved in my wonderful wife.

• • • • •

I still volunteered and worked part-time at Destination Church in Virginia. Shannon visited the church with me, and although her first impressions were less than glowing, she quickly grew to like the lack of pretension and the genuineness of the T-shirt crowd showing up to learn more about Jesus.

Meanwhile, I was also refereeing basketball games, working with our family construction company, working with Marriage Helper, and working as a leadership coach with the popular author and speaker John Maxwell, known around the world for his books and seminars for individuals, companies, and other organizations. I was busy! We finally had some sporadic but steady income, so that provided more options for us.

When I talked to Joe Beam regarding Marriage Helper workshops, he indicated that his schedule had slowed a bit. "That's fine," I said. "Just let me know if or when you need me."

Pastor Brian was delighted to put me on retainer to help the Destination staff. The church was loosely associated with the Assemblies of God, I had discovered, since Brian was technically an Assemblies pastor and part of the ARC, the denomination's church-planting organization.

Occasionally, when telling someone else about me, Brian would refer to me as Destination's executive pastor. I appreciated his confidence, but I quickly corrected him. "Don't call me pastor," I said. "I'm not a pastor."

Brian possessed a marvelous attitude of grace, so he thought it was funny when I balked at being labeled. When he introduced me to new friends, he often said, "The first thing Jimmy told me was that he did not want to be a pastor."

Yet there I was at Destination, speaking from the platform again. People in the congregation often called me Pastor Jim, and I'd quickly remind them, "No, I'm just helping. I'm not a pastor." But they had assimilated me into a pastoral role, so people automatically assumed that I was a pastor.

When I hedged about being called a pastor, Brian smiled knowingly. "You have God-given gifts, and you need to use them," he said. He encouraged me to reach out to the denominational leaders and seek to be relicensed as a minister. I was reluctant, but Brian convinced me that I could better serve at Destination as well as other smaller churches if I were officially endorsed by the denominational leadership.

I petitioned the national office of the Assemblies of God to be reordained. I met with and was interviewed by the leaders and took a series of psychological examinations regarding my fitness for ministry—a bit of irony to me, considering my history with Jimmy Swaggart, a leading Assemblies of God minister who had so adamantly opposed Christian psychology.

Because I had resigned my position at the church in Massachusetts and hadn't been removed by either the church leadership or the denominational hierarchy, it was an easier process to be reinstated as an ordained pastor. I still had no desire to lead a congregation, so my reason for wanting to be reinstated was so I could be licensed and more officially serve with Destination and other Assemblies of God churches. I knew I had some skills in church growth principles, so I thought I could be of assistance to some smaller congregations that wanted to increase their numbers and influence in their communities.

I soon discovered, however, that unlike Pastor Briggs at Destination, most of the leaders in those smaller churches did not really want help or were afraid of bringing in an "outside consultant"—namely, me. It wasn't so much that they had heard about my personal failures; they simply had their own things going on. They didn't want anyone rocking their boats. They didn't want to spend the money or take any risks. After all, church coups were not uncommon. Consequently, although the leaders were frustrated and disappointed, most of the pastors with whom I conferred preferred to cater to what the people in the congregation wanted, whether it was a positive program or not. That wasn't unusual; indeed, many of the same problems exist in most churches, regardless of size. But I couldn't help them if they were unwilling to change the status quo, so I temporarily gave up on that possibility.

During that time, I had begun traveling with Marriage Helper again, often sharing our story during the workshops. I also spoke at Destination church ten to twelve times per year, usually when Brian was on vacation or traveling for ministry. We planned the year's services in advance, so I knew the subject and content we were going to address. That made it easier for me to fill in whenever Pastor Brian needed me. Most of our messages were topic driven. Rather than simply discussing things that interested us, our goal was to answer questions that people were asking. That's why people showed up.

The freestyle church pioneered by Pastor Brian Briggs and his wife, Kelly, where many people in the group were covered with tattoos and piercings and we all served each other, continued to thrive. I served at Destination Church for about two and a half years, but more and more I ruminated on developing my own speaking business.

It was a major indication of the improvement in Shannon's and my relationship and the way we communicated that I didn't merely pick up and quit the job. I wanted to talk it over with my wife. Shannon believed in me so much that she left her parents' home and what little security she had remaining, so for me to now inform her that I wanted to launch out on my own, starting my own company, was another stretch for her. I introduced the subject slowly and gave Shannon plenty of time to speak into the decision and offer her opinions and insights.

When Shannon and I discussed my potential future employment as part of the Destination Church staff, I was honest with her. "This is not what I wanted to do," I said to Shannon. "I just wanted to help. I'm not comfortable performing a pastoral function. I'm not 'spiritual' enough or willing to attempt being 'the image of God' for other people. I can't keep doing this." Part of my reluctance, of course, was because I didn't want to fail anyone. I wanted to be a regular guy. In a pastoral position, I felt that I would fail. I didn't fit the pastoral mode. My response to that was simply to express more bravado, which tended to produce a counterproductive, rebellious spirit within me. That wasn't good for the congregation or for Shannon and me.

On the other hand, Pastor Brian had been exceptionally kind to me, and the church had been good to us. They provided steady income, insurance benefits, and freedom to try new ideas. It wasn't that I felt I couldn't do the job; I simply did not want that responsibility. I met with Pastor Brian, explained my reasoning, and resigned my position at Destination church.

But what was I going to do? I had to make a living. But my heart was not in working with my brother or father in construction, and as much as I appreciated John Maxwell's motivating leadership principles, I wanted to make the most of the lessons I had learned the hard way. Scripture promises that God will take even our embarrassing and painful experiences and use them to help someone else if we will allow Him to do that.

Can He still do something with me, I wondered, *that might help other struggling couples?*

RENEWED TRUST

CHAPTER 31

WHO, ME?
A MARRIAGE HELPER?

S hannon and I had been back together barely a year when I met with Dr. Joe Beam again and spoke with him and his daughter, Kimberly, who had taken over more of the marketing responsibilities for Marriage Helper. After a brief conversation and catching up with each other, I presented an idea I had been ruminating on: "Shannon and I know how tough it was for us to apply all that we learned at the workshop on our own. We could make Marriage Helper even stronger if we provided a coaching program for people who have completed a weekend workshop and are now looking for some long-term help."

"Great idea," Joe said. "Can you develop that?"

I smiled. "I'm pretty sure that I can."

I went to work designing a coaching program to help people who have gone through Marriage Helper. The program offered both immediate guidance and long-term follow-up materials to encourage couples to continue working on their "new" marriage and to help keep couples accountable. In the process, we discovered that the coaching program could help even those who had never been to a weekend workshop.

I enjoyed developing the coaching program for Marriage Helper, so it simply made sense to Dr. Joe and Kimberly to have me lead it. Joe was more of a visionary than an administrative sort of guy, so the Marriage Helper board of directors cast their eyes on Joe's daughter, Kimberly Holmes, to run the organization. Besides bringing a bright, young, female perspective to Marriage Helper, Kimberly also brought a wealth of marketing knowledge. She became the CEO and is a tremendous asset to the program.

As for me, I was in my lane. Rather than being a headliner at Marriage Helper workshops, I could function well behind the scenes as a coach, the encourager behind the key players as well as the people who attended the events. Of course, Joe also wanted me to speak during the workshop sessions or small group breakouts. At first I spoke only occasionally at Marriage Helper workshops and only when Joe asked me to do so. Then, little by little, Joe put me on the platform more frequently. Before long I was helping him carry the entire weekend workshop load, but I remained a "guest speaker." I wasn't officially part of the organization.

For me, the best part of working with Marriage Helper was watching people change within the course of a three-day workshop. Many couples walk into the sessions barely speaking to each other. But they find hope of transformation through the workshops.

Some people don't make it, and I can't always predict who will or won't be able to save their marriage. Sometimes even I am surprised. In an extreme case, a teacher had an affair with a seventeen-year-old girl. He went to prison, but when he got out, he and his wife attended our workshop and were able to work together to restore their marriage. Who would have guessed that? Not me.

But since then I've witnessed thousands of couples in dire straits who have been able to build a new marriage, the marriage they want.

In many cases, the burden for success in reconnection often depends on the spouse who has not or is not having the affair. Why? Because the person who is having the affair is usually not interested in saving the marriage. He or she does not want the relationship to work. After studying a twenty-five-year literature review of materials written on marriage and divorce, renown marriage researcher Dr. John Gottman concluded that the most common reasons for divorce include, "I don't feel you love me," "I don't feel you like me," and "I don't feel you respect me." Often, those feelings grow out of a lack of acceptance: "I don't feel that you accept me" or "I don't accept myself" or both. After more than twenty-five years of researching the reasons marriages fall apart, I am convinced this is true: lacking like, love, and respect are even more frequently the cause of divorce than money issues, parenting problems, or even affairs.

On the other hand, there are some character traits, attitudes, and behaviors that commonly lead to failure rather than success. For instance, a survey was conducted that asked couples why they remained committed to their marriage or the relationship they were in, basically asking, "Why are you still in the marriage?"

The answers fell into three main categories. (1) An internal choice: "I *want* to stay in this relationship, regardless." (2) An internal value system: I *ought* to; in other words, "Because of my beliefs and values, I really should do this." That sort of choice is based more on commitment than intimacy. (3) The third reason people stay in a relationship is constraint: "I *have* to do this; I don't really have a choice. It is my obligation." We often joke with some couples that in their background, murder might be acceptable but divorce is anathema. Sometimes, though, this third reason may indicate that the person feels there are no viable alternatives other than remaining in a bad marriage. For instance, a man may feel he is too old to find someone else, or too unattractive, or that his best years are behind him, so he assumes that he cannot attract another woman, and he will stay in the relationship regardless of how poorly he is treated.

A man I coached was married to a woman who had twenty-seven affairs yet he stayed married to her. When I asked him why he stayed with his adulterous wife, his response surprised and saddened me. "Of all her affairs, only seventeen of them were physical; the others were emotional," he said.

"Okay, I admire your commitment," I said, "but why are you still there?"

He looked at me plaintively and tears filled his eyes. He raised his hand and pointed to his face and then down to his body. "Who is going to want to be with me?" he asked. "At least I have somebody occasionally."

I melted in shared pain with a man who felt he had nowhere to go and nobody to love him except a perpetually adulterous woman. That is not a good place to live.

The only place in which we really feel good is "the want-to stage," when we stay in a relationship because we want to. The other two stages, the ought-to and have-to areas, will not lead to intimacy, no matter how hard a couple tries. A healthy marriage thrives in the "want to" place. The husband and wife want to be together and are willing to do whatever it takes—even if that requires change— to speak to one's spouse in a manner that he or she relates to and to put the other person's needs ahead of your own. That kind of marriage can withstand the storms of life that are sure to assail us all.

· · · · ·

For five years Joe and Kimberly talked to me about moving to Tennessee to work full-time with them. Knowing that Joe was quick to acknowledge that he was not an administrative sort of guy, I didn't want to assume that responsibility, so I turned him down repeatedly. I was concerned that I was not the "right guy at the right time." But when Kimberly became the CEO of Marriage Helper and the structure of the organization could accommodate more growth, it made more sense for Shannon and me to move. Joe could set the vision, Kimberly could run the operation, and I could do the workshops and coach people wanting to save or improve their marriage. In September 2019, Shannon and I moved to Tennessee and I joined forces with Dr. Joe and Kimberly full-time. Eventually I became director of operations for Marriage Helper and worked to restructure the organization. I designed and headed up the coaching department and continued to develop materials couples could use to improve their relationships. Before long, I became the senior coach and facilitated many of the weekend workshops. Now it was me standing before a room full of couples harboring fragile hope that their marriage could be restored. It was me telling the story of how our marriage nearly dissolved in divorce. And it was me offering hope that if our marriage could be saved, so can yours.

It wasn't easy. When I first started conducting workshops for Joe, I quit almost every month. "I just can't do it, Joe," I whined. "I feel like such a hypocrite. My marriage isn't strong enough yet. I can't be a role model. I'm a screwup!"

"You're doing fine," Joe countered. "There are no perfect relationships, and we're all screwups, so join the club."

Joe's compassionate, encouraging attitude was so different from that of other leaders with whom I'd worked in various places. He was not stingy about sharing stage time or possessively worried that the workshop participants might like me more than him. He was confident in his own abilities and wanted the best for all of us. Although I knew every workshop was crucial in the lives of the couples attending, I didn't feel that I had to earn their acceptance. Joe accepted me; he believed in me, and he had been helping couples for a long time. If Joe trusted me and had confidence in me, I could go into a workshop knowing that what I had to offer mattered.

Still, it took some getting used to.

Shannon and I had attended only one workshop as a couple, and although I had spent hundreds of hours in study and months in training with Dr. Joe, now I was suddenly back up on the platform telling others how they could improve their lives. I was still struggling with *me* and how to deal with my own pain, often attempting to mask it or push it down inside me somewhere. I still made poor decisions regarding my relationship with Shannon. I recognized the dangers of that and didn't want to mislead or hurt anyone else, especially since my wife and I were still relearning how to function as a married couple ourselves. We were back together, but we weren't in heaven yet.

We were still grappling with what John Gottman refers to as "The Four Horseman" of communication styles: criticism, contempt, defensiveness, and stonewalling. Alluding to the "Four Horsemen of the Apocalypse" (Revelation 6:1–8), conquest, war, hunger, and death, Gottman contends that in his research, he discovered that if married couples can eliminate the communication "four horsemen" from their conversations and replace them with healthy communication patterns, they can lower the risk of divorce by eighty-two percent. Shannon and I were still working on those.

---

* Gottman, John Mordechai, and Nan Silver. *The Seven Principles for Making Marriage Work*, 45. New York: Harmony Books, 2015.

When speaking at Marriage Helper events, rather than attempting to perpetuate the myth that we had it all together, I honestly admitted that I sometimes used criticism or contempt in my conversations with Shannon. "There have been times when I would put down my wife, just to make myself feel better," I confessed. "Of course, when I did that, she became defensive and simply shut down emotionally as well as conversationally, stonewalling any further discussion. That was wrong of me and unhealthy, and I had to find better ways to communicate with her."

I cautioned the workshop participants, "Don't mistake habit for a heart issue. After Shannon and I were reunited and were learning about Gottman's four horsemen, my heart had changed but I was still a creature of habit. I told her, 'I recognize how destructive those negative forms of communication are, so I don't want to criticize you or use contempt in my conversations with you anymore.' But then something would set me off, and I would fall back on my old habits, using put-downs and other contemptible language in my conversations with her. That was the habit speaking but not my heart. My heart had genuinely changed, but my habits had not yet caught up.

"Regardless of your good intentions," I told the group, "or how high of a religious experience you have, or any other sort of epiphany, it takes time to replace an old habit with a new, better one. You have to extend a lot of grace to each other as you realize that your partner has changed but is still overcoming negative habits. But if that pattern continues, you must confront it, albeit gently, and not in the middle of an argument. Try not to judge the intent of your spouse's habitual conduct or conversation. With time, and the establishment of new patterns, together you can change the behavior for the better."

Despite my feelings of inadequacy, I enjoyed sharing what I was learning with the workshop participants. Perhaps because I was so transparent about my own failures, many of them found renewed hope that their marriage could be regenerated.

For her part, Shannon wasn't interested in speaking at the workshops or in any other public setting. Although she loved meeting and talking with the attendees on a one-to-one basis, she didn't consider herself a public speaker or a spokesperson for Marriage Helper. Still, people wanted to know what Shannon had experienced and what she had felt. "How did you take care of your mind?" they wanted to know. "How did you forgive your husband?" they asked. "How long did it take?" One of my personal favorites that women asked Shannon was, "Did you ever want to beat up the other girl?"

"Yes," she answered honestly, although she never did, and even apologized to Vanessa for treating her unkindly, all the while suspecting that her friend was having an affair with me. Most of all, both men and women wanted to know why Shannon hadn't left me.

We found that the best way to answer those kinds of questions was to do a workshop session on Sunday in which the participants could ask Shannon any question. Nothing was off-limits, and it was a no-holds-barred atmosphere. Shannon fielded the queries like a pro, and the workshop attendees appreciated her straightforward, down-to-earth honesty.

In the workshops we talked a lot about avoiding "pushes," saying or doing those things that will push a spouse further away or possibly even out the door. As Shannon instinctively knew about me, had she vehemently criticized or castigated me about my infidelity to her, I most likely would have walked out the door and not have come back. But because she didn't do those things and we remained together, there were opportunities for her to show me that she still loved me and that she had not given up on our marriage. That may not have happened had she engaged in "pushes" that made it easier for me to leave and not look back. The fact that she had not pushed me out the door, or built fences I needed to hurdle to get back into her good graces, made my return to our marriage less awkward.

In the workshops, I especially enjoyed trying to answer questions couples were really asking instead of simply providing a seminar or lecture on what I thought might benefit them. One question that came up frequently was, "Am I condoning an affair if I don't push back on my spouse? In other words, does my trying to be a nice person imply that I don't care what my marriage partner has done and is continuing to do?"

The simple answer is, "No, refusing to become belligerent does not mean that you condone your spouse's behavior." It means that you are committed to being a kind person. Like Shannon, you may be operating on the principle "Be still and know that I am God." You accept the person, faults and all, knowing that we all fall short and believing that by finding the true reasons for your spouse's infidelity, you can move forward and hopefully save your marriage.

CHAPTER 32

So, What Can I Do?

I f it doesn't help to gripe, complain, rebuke, or push your spouse further away, what *can* you do?

At a workshop where that question came up, I told people, "If you want to save your marriage from divorce, even if your spouse is involved in an affair, don't start by throwing out accusations and remonstrations. Start by working on yourself."

I could tell by looking into the faces in front of me that what I was saying was not the popular answer or the message they expected to hear. But I continued, "If you have recently discovered that your spouse is having an affair or wants out of your marriage, that can be an extremely disconcerting time. After all, you've invested in that relationship. You've loved deeply; you've tried, and perhaps you are confused. Can your relationship be saved?

"Yes, there is hope. Over the years, I've seen hundreds of marriages saved and the relationships restored. It can happen for you as well.

"But there are a few things you must do. First, *do everything you can to become the best version of you that is possible.*

"Start by working on what Marriage Helper refers to as your PIES, the physical, intellectual, emotional, and spiritual parts of yourself. In good relationships, those things usually start out positively, but over time, we can neglect our PIES and they can go neutral or, worse, become negatives. When you first met your partner, there was an attraction between the two of you. Your spouse was attracted to you because he or she thought you were in a good place and a person that they wanted to be around. But if your marriage is in trouble, consider this: your spouse may be thinking that your lack of care for your PIES shows a lack of love and respect for him or her. So you have to work on you. The good news is, if that person was attracted to you once, your partner can be attracted to you again. Rather than trying to change your spouse, start by changing *you*.

"Attraction to another person is much more than physical appearance, but appearance does matter. Work on your physical body to get into the best shape possible for your age.

"Similarly, work on your intellectual and emotional growth, and place your spiritual life as a priority. Intellectual growth doesn't necessarily mean you must be book smart, but it does require that you continue to grow your mind and learn new things in areas you can share with your partner, things you can talk about and simply enjoy doing together. Put down your phone and get off social media and talk to your partner.

"Emotional attraction is perhaps the most important element in a relationship. It doesn't mean that you are perpetually lovey-dovey. It means that you evoke emotions and feelings in the other person that he or she enjoys feeling. So work on those things that cause you to feel better about yourself, but also work on what causes your spouse to feel better about himself or herself.

"Spiritual attraction has to do with beliefs and values even more than religion or faith. Most people enjoy being together with others who have similar beliefs and values. So work on developing those, defining what you really believe and knowing better who you are. Then live consistently with what you believe.

"Second, *lead your thoughts*. When you learn that your spouse is having an affair or wants out of the marriage, it can become an emotional explosion. The natural reaction is to want to act or react in some decisive, profound, or retaliatory manner that will have an impact on your spouse. But acting on emotional impulse will not get you the results you hope to obtain. If you are hurt, anxious, or angry about what your spouse has done, you are not going to think well. Instead, try to pause, take a breath—or possibly a number of deep breaths—and try to collect your thoughts. Think through this. Choose to lead your thoughts rather than allowing your thoughts to drive you. Yes, this infidelity is a threat to your well-being, but if you respond with vengeance at an emotional level, your actions may be counterproductive to restoring your marriage in the long term.

"Third, *focus on the right now*. Certainly, down the road, in evaluating your relationship, you will want to consider the long-term impact of the affair or the desire to leave the marriage. But in the immediate aftermath of such revelations, it is best to look carefully at what you are doing *today* to have a positive impact on your spouse. What you do today will produce what will happen tomorrow. If you are fighting with your spouse, trying to prove your point, or firing emotional shots, it will only create a larger rift between you and your partner rather than creating a better connection. You already have the rift; you don't need more of that. Again, the most important question you can ask yourself is, 'What do I need to change right now?' Focus on that.

"Ask yourself, 'Am I a safe place emotionally for my spouse, so when my partner shares secrets or deep, emotional pain with me, I don't attack? Instead, I listen and truly hear my spouse.'

"Fourth, accept the fact that some things will go wrong, so you need to *be flexible*. You probably had a lot of little things that led to the degradation of your relationship, and they are not going to improve overnight. Those small things add up. You have to take small steps to change behavior so you are drawing your spouse toward you rather than pushing your partner away.

"It is important to be flexible. Once the subject of divorce comes up, people tend to become rigid. They draw lines that they do not want crossed. Be careful. As Andy Stanley, a leadership mentor of mine often said, 'Be careful about making your point. You might make a point and not make a difference.' You want to make a difference in your relationship. You want your spouse to see you differently, more accurately in the place and love that you have for your marriage partner. Compromise is the key.

"Fifth, listen to understand, not merely to challenge or comment on what your spouse has said. Attempt to honestly hear the other person. Be prepared to ask questions of your spouse when you don't understand. *What are you saying?* Don't assume that your understanding of certain words is identical to that of your spouse. Ask questions that help both of you to communicate more clearly.

"Sixth, revisit your PIES often. Falling in love is as easy as PIES," I quipped. But then I quickly drove home my point. "If you spend your time and energy focusing on the pain in your relationship, you will miss the opportunity to improve yourself. But if you center your attention on improving yourself, if and when your spouse returns, you will be a better person and better prepared to create a better marriage. Get ready now for the day your spouse comes back rather than merely trying to figure out what went wrong in your relationship. If your PIES are healthy, everything about you will be more attractive, your decisions will be healthy, your daily walk will be more healthy, and that is a good place to be as you try to influence your spouse."

• • • • •

During one workshop, an attractive woman who looked to be in her late thirties or early forties voiced a question to me that others were probably thinking as well. She said, "My husband has cheated on me several times with various women. I've been working on myself, praying, and asking God for wisdom. What more can I do?"

"There's always something more you can do," I said, "but sometimes even doing the right thing at the wrong time will produce a negative result."

The look on her face told me that my statement was confusing to her.

"If you plant a seed, water it, fertilize it, and care for it, but then a few weeks later you dig it up to see how the seed is doing, what will happen?"

"The plant will probably die," she said.

"Right, and that's what happens when we don't allow the positive seed you plant in the relationship to grow to fruition. As it breaks through the ground, you can nurture it, protect it, and treat it for bugs as you need to. You respond to the growth of the seed. But if you dig up the seed to see how it is growing, you thwart any progress that you have made. Sometimes you must simply wait, believe for the best, and pray; and yes, sometimes you give respect to someone who doesn't deserve it yet. Some things simply take time. But the alternative is to prematurely dig up what you have planted. I'm not saying it is easy, and most of us have to ask God to help us be patient. But seeing a strong, healthy plant is worth it."

• • • • •

Sometimes people want to do too much. "Don't commit to doing anything you aren't able to continue," I tell people that I coach. I once had a woman say that she was going to write her husband a love note every day for the rest of her life.

I said, "Whoa! You might want to reconsider that. Who could do that? Three hundred and sixty-five notes in just one year? I couldn't think of that many good things to say to anybody! So perhaps you may want to tone that statement back a bit, to avoid unrealistic expectations. Start now to realistically do what adds value and what brings love, like, and respect to your relationship, and do it consistently, without expectation of reciprocation, and receiving a return."

Keep in mind: you can't change anyone else; you can only change yourself. Moreover, it will be counterproductive in your marriage if you attempt to coerce your spouse into doing something he or she doesn't want to do. You can't force your partner to stay nor can you prevent that person from leaving.

But with your newly improved physical health, intellectual awareness, emotional stability, and spiritual growth, you are clearly stating, "It's in both our best interests to stay and work on this marriage. If you decide to leave, you're going to miss this."

CHAPTER 33

LIMERENCE—
THE LITTLE-KNOWN LURE

One of the keys that helped me come to my senses and changed our marriage was discovering an understanding of limerence. Like many other people, neither of us had ever heard the word before I had an affair. Nor had I ever encountered the concept prior to attending the Marriage Helper workshop. *Limerence? What is that?* I wondered as Dr. Beam described his own limerent experience in the first Marriage Helper workshop Shannon and I attended. In Joe's case, he was in limerence for more than three years, and it cost him his marriage and his relationship with his children. He and his wife actually divorced. But eventually they got back together and their family was restored. Not everyone is so fortunate.

As for me, I thought that I was in love with Vanessa. What I actually plunged into headlong was limerence.

"So what is limerence?" I'll ask in a workshop. "Many of you are probably unfamiliar with the term, yet you may be surprised to discover that you are involved in a limerent relationship. I certainly was!"

I explain, "Limerence is when a person becomes romantically infatuated with another, mentally and emotionally dwelling on him or her almost constantly in hopes of having those feelings reciprocated. It is that intense desire to possess another person completely with what is assumed to be love. 'I want to build my life around you,' the limerent lover declares to his or her partner. Often, this is an unrealistic dream, but that doesn't matter. To the person caught up in limerence, he or she can see only the good qualities of the person to whom they are attracted. We call that 'the halo effect,' seeing only the good and rejecting the negative qualities or circumstances of the person or relationship."

So in every workshop, I talk about the difference between love and limerence. I begin by presenting a bit of background information and context. "The word was coined in the 1970s by psychologist Dr. Dorothy Tennov to identify people in the state of attraction in which they think they are in 'madly in love'—but are not really," I tell workshop participants. Tennov wrote a book, *Love and Limerence: The Experience of Being in Love*, based on her study of relationships. To be fair, I inform our clients, "Most marriage counselors were never taught about limerence in college, so you should know that many clinical psychologists and marriage counselors initially discounted Dr. Tennov's ideas as unscientific or implausible. But they offered no alternatives other than to keep seeking 'true love,' through traditional marriage counseling, which was often ineffective.

"Years later, Dr. Helen Fisher, an anthropological biologist, studied the brains of people who claimed to be deeply in love, and she examined what actually happens in the brain when someone is convinced that he or she is in love. She discovered that dopamine increases in the brain as the person dwells on the other person with whom they think they are in love, creating good feelings. Serotonin decreases, creating an ecstasy-agony cycle of roller-coaster feelings—ecstasy because the person wants to be with me, then agony because maybe the person is moving away from me. This intense feeling of limerence is produced by chemicals in the brain and is a temporary condition, but it often causes a person to leave his or her spouse and children to pursue a relationship with another person with whom they *think* they are in love. While it may have spiritual causes as well, the primary causes are chemical and emotional. The limerent person becomes afraid that the relationship will end, and the fear intensifies the passion.

"When you or your spouse say, 'I'm in love with another person, and that person is not you,' is that really true love? Often, it is not. It is limerence. While limerence is a real form of love, it is similar to 'puppy love' between two teenagers. It is a real form of love, albeit immature, but it is not the lasting, mature, complete form of love most people hope to find in a marriage partner."

During the workshops, I also invest time in discussing true intimacy. Many people who are involved in an affair think they are experiencing "intimacy" for the first time, or the first time in a long time, because they are physically "one" with their partner.

"I've never been able to talk to anyone so openly and honestly like this," Julie said about the man with whom she was having an affair. "Curt really understands me. We're so close. He believes in me. I've never told anyone these kinds of things before."

No, that's not really true. Curt simply doesn't disagree with her because he is viewing everything she says or does through a "halo effect." True intimacy cannot exist when one or both members are looking at each other and seeing that halo effect in which their partners can say or do no wrong. It is as though she is saying something as foolish as, "I know he robs banks for a living, but he is such a good guy at heart, and he promised that he would stop robbing banks for me." That's ludicrous!

"You are overlooking the person's flaws because you are so caught up in the affair," I tell audiences. "You're just seeing the good stuff. So it is not a true intimacy. True intimacy is looking at the other person and finding acceptance even in our disagreement. That occurs only in safety, and the safest place to find that sort of acceptance is in a loving marriage relationship."

What makes a person vulnerable to limerence? It usually affects people who feel that they are missing something in their marriage relationship. Moreover, limerence can often be traced to something that happened in a person's childhood. If his or her parents divorced, or a person grew up with a lack of acceptance or had an intense need to feel love or significance, those experiences can create a predisposition toward limerence. The person may long to know that he or she has value and significance, yet people can rarely pinpoint these longings. As unusual as it may seem, some people may not even be aware of these feelings, yet they influence every relationship in their lives. Some wonder, *Am I even a lovable person?*

Does this sound familiar? It sure did to me.

For two single individuals, the initial attraction created by limerence *can* be a positive experience, especially when their intense attraction leads to marriage. But if you or your partner are involved with someone who is bad for you or is committed to another partner, that relationship is bound to be destructive. Nearly two-thirds of the people who attend the Marriage Helper workshops have had at least one affair. Some have had multiple affairs. For some, the affair is simply about sex. But for many others, it is not so much about the sex but rather about distorted dreams of a relationship.

"Limerence always ends," I tell workshop participants. "Maybe not today, or next month, but it will end. It has a limited shelf life. You can be certain of that."

Most relationships based in limerence end somewhere between three months and three years, and few last longer than forty-eight months before the couple breaks up. Dr. Tennov felt certain that most limerent relationships are shorter than that—somewhere between six months and two years.

Even for limerent couples who have an affair, divorce their spouses, and marry each other (surprisingly, only one in ten limerent couples will actually marry the partner with whom they are having the affair), the numbers are not in their favor. Of those couples who marry, over ninety percent will divorce within five years. Those who remain married are outliers who defy the odds.

"Marriage Helper's founder, Dr. Joe Beam, has identified three stages of limerence, the first being *infatuation*," I told a workshop group. "Similar to infatuation in other sorts of love, this is often the initial attraction between two people. The second phase Dr. Joe describes as *crystallization*, when the person becomes obsessed with the idea that the relationship is really going to work out; then the third phase is *deterioration*, when the relationship begins to crumble.

"Interestingly, while an affair may seem to energize a person for a while, limerence actually causes a person's productivity to decrease and often to disappear entirely. He or she may spend inappropriate amounts of time online or on social media, texting or sending emails back and forth, spending as much as 85 percent of the day thinking about their love interest. You can guess what that does to efficiency in the workplace, so not surprisingly, there are often negative business or employment ramifications of an affair.

"So what can you do," I asked the workshop participants, "if your spouse has had an affair or is even currently involved in an affair?"

Most of the participants stared back at me blankly, as though to say, "That's why we came here—to find out what we could do."

My next statement usually surprises people.

"Don't worry so much about where your spouse is," I advise, "or what he or she is doing, but center on your behavior, developing your PIES and doing the things that add value to your life. Look at it this way: You are going to expend energy over this relationship somehow. So rather than focusing on your spouse's actions and failures—over which you have little to no control—why not focus on *you* and improving the part of your behavior that may have led to a break in intimacy? You will be a stronger, more confident person as a result."

CHAPTER 34

Is There Hope?

A question I often hear from most spouses I am coaching and often heard at Marriage Helper workshops is, "Is there hope?" Or, as the corollary to that question, I've often heard a spouse say, "I don't want to have false hope."

To me, there is no such thing as "false hope." Certainly, nobody wants to have blind, misguided, foolish, or naive hope. Shelly's husband, Brad, was unfaithful and mean to her for more than six months. But suddenly, overnight, he began treating her with exceptional kindness.

Shelly was excited. "Maybe he's turning around!" she gushed to me.

"Stop," I told her bluntly. "Yes, have hope that he is going to change, but if you are assuming that after six months of being a demon he has suddenly turned into a saint, that's probably not what happened." That is blind or naive hope.

On the other hand, I understand that the person doesn't want to be deceived or encouraged to continue a relationship that is over, but as long as there is genuine hope, the relationship is not over.

A further question is, "Can you keep hope alive?"

Are you able to stay engaged in the process of improving your marriage? Some people focus on the events going on in their relationship. "We got in a fight last week." That isn't really the problem so much as a symptom of how the couple is thinking.

What are you focusing on? If you focus on the behaviors of the other person rather than the potential of the relationship, you will always find the negative.

Similarly, when we talk about the "what ifs," we usually go to the negative. But if we can turn that around, it can directly affect the relationship.

"Right now, I don't have hope," a guy whose wife wanted a divorce told me.

"Okay, but do you think about the past or the future potential?" I asked. "You want the relationship to work, so listen to that voice in your head and heart. Ingest positive thoughts into your mind on a daily basis."

Some people read all sorts of books about marriage but then become disillusioned when they compare their situation to others or attempt to apply some of those principles in their own relationship and are frustrated over their inability to make those things work. Certainly, you should educate yourself about how to communicate better and how to deal with priority matters in your marriage, but keep your focus on the positive things you can do, and don't compare your relationship to other people or the ideals you read about or hear discussed. As long as you and your spouse are alive, there is always hope.

I've had people tell me, "We are getting a divorce. We will sign the papers next week, so I guess the marriage is over."

I don't accept that. I tell my clients, "Divorce is an event. That's all. Don't make your decisions based only on an event. Unless one of you is dying or one of you is remarried to someone other than your original spouse, as long as you are still breathing, there is always hope."

But hope depends on what you decide to do. Even if the divorce documents are signed and completed, a couple can still be reunited if they will begin behaviors that positively affect their future. In my talks, I remind struggling couples of Dr. Joe Beam and his wife, Alice, who divorced for three years but got back together and decided to do things differently. They remarried each other and are still living in love to this day.

Over the years, I've coached numerous couples who have chosen to believe that divorce is not the final word. It's never easy, but it is possible.

I could tell Scott and his wife, Ruth, were in trouble the moment I saw them at a workshop where I was a breakout leader. Scott was a widower raising three children as a single dad. He had met Ruth, a resident of Guatemala, a single mom with a four-year-old child, when he had participated in a missions trip to her country in 2004. Ruth and Scott married and blended their families shortly thereafter. Both of them had strong Christian backgrounds, so they served in a college ministry in Colorado.

They were married for seven years when the bottom fell out and Ruth opened her heart to a relationship outside the marriage. Scott confronted her with an ultimatum—something we don't recommend—and told her, "You can have our marriage or you can have your boyfriend, but you can't have both. You need to choose."

Ruth chose to leave the marriage a week later. She was convinced that God would not want her to be unhappy. Friends tried to remind Ruth of the Scripture she believed. But she didn't want to hear it. Indeed, their efforts put her off even more.

Still, Scott refused to give up on their marriage. He continued to believe that they could be reunited. In the meantime, he went on with his life, worked on his PIES, and took care of himself. It took a year and a half for him to convince Ruth to attend a Marriage Helper workshop with him. Ruth finally agreed to attend the workshop only so Scott would stop contesting their divorce.

Following the main sessions, Ruth told Scott, "Thank you for insisting that we attend the workshop. I learned a lot, but I'm asking you to respect my decision." She said, "Scott, I know what you want, but it would take a miracle for us to have a chance to get back together."

During the final breakout session, as a concluding question, I asked the attendees, "What do you think God would have you do about your marriage, or if you are not a person of faith, what do your core beliefs and values tell you to do?"

With tears in his eyes, Scott stood up, and with Ruth in the room, said, "I believe I am to release my wife and our marriage to God and to let the outcome up to Him."

I was deeply moved by Scott's response. I looked at him and said, "Bro, that is exactly right. That is the best thing you can do right now in your situation."

The couple left the workshop, and five days later their divorce was finalized—at least as far as the lawyers and the state were concerned.

Ruth, too, was convinced that she could find happiness in her new relationship. She conceived a child, but when it came time for her to give birth, the father of the child was AWOL. Ruth called Scott and asked if he would come to the hospital because her water had broken and she was anticipating delivery that night. Scott didn't hesitate. He remembered our counsel, "Be a safe place for her," so he hurried to the hospital to be with his former wife—who was about to give birth to another man's child.

Soon, Scott looked into the face of a beautiful baby girl named Valentina, wrapped in a blanket in a bassinet. "Valentina, you are beautiful like your mother," he said. "I'm so glad you are here. Welcome to our world. Happy birthday; I love you."

About eight months later, Ruth called Scott at 5:00 a.m. He could barely understand what she was saying because she was crying so hysterically. "Baby . . . fever . . . please pray," were the only words that Scott could make out. But he raced to the house, where he found Valentina racked with a 104.5-degree fever. Ruth had been up all night with her, trying to get the fever under control, to no avail.

Scott prayed a simple prayer for the desperately sick child to be healed. When the prayer was over, Valentina sat up, looked at Ruth and Scott, and smiled. Her clothing was soaked, but her fever was gone; her forehead was cool.

Later that night, Scott returned to Ruth's home to check on them, and Valentina was perfectly fine. "Ruth, do you know what happened this morning?" Scott asked.

"Yes, that was amazing," Ruth responded.

Scott said, "What happened this morning was that you got your miracle."

Ruth realized that God had answered her prayers, not only for Valentina but for herself to be loved. She later said, "Even though I would not admit it, I knew that what I was doing was wrong the whole time." But no human being could convince her of that; only God could. And He did.

Ruth and Scott returned to the workshop in 2017, this time as a divorced couple exploring the possibility of reconciliation. When Scott suggested attending the workshop again, Ruth responded, "I'm willing to go again because I felt respected the first time we attended."

A year later, the couple attended a third Marriage Helper workshop, this time as a newly engaged couple. They left the workshop early on Sunday afternoon so they could get remarried on September 23, 2018. It wasn't fairy-tale or Hollywood, but they got back together based on their desires to do the right things. Their reuniting was based not so much on feeling as it was on belief. Their want-to followed their ought-to, their desire to do the right things.

Today, they are more in love than they were when they first married. Valentina is a well-adjusted little girl, growing up in a home with two loving parents. The couple succeeded in putting their relationship on a good track, and today Scott is one of my most effective marriage coaches. This couple is living proof that there is hope, even after a divorce or some other negative event.

After an event, take the next thirty days or so and evaluate how you feel about it. Were your emotions explosive? Did they remind you of something else—perhaps a previous relationship or even your own parents' marriage? Seek out a qualified marriage coach or counselor whose client is *the marriage* and who will respect you as an individual. You don't have to do this alone, but be careful: don't take the opinions or advice of unqualified people too seriously, not even those of your closest friends. Most likely, your friends will mirror your own thoughts and opinions and tell you what you want to hear rather than what you might need to hear. You'll do better if you process your feelings with wise, professional counselors.

Can you instill hope in a spouse? That is difficult, but you can influence your spouse, either positively or negatively. Find a way to build the positive, adding value to the other person or enhancing positive emotions. Provide an alternative view, a new vision of your marriage's potential. Don't waste your time trying to resurrect a dead relationship. That "old marriage" is dead, so focus your energy on the possibilities for you and your spouse that are ahead of you, and concentrate on demonstrating the kind of behavior that will build a positively improved new version of your marriage.

Don't allow anything about your behavior to create negative emotions in your spouse. Even when your spouse does not respond positively, you still have a choice who you will be and how you will react. Sure, you may want to respond to negative actions or words by your spouse with an equal and opposite reaction, but you don't need to do that. If you know you are going to have a difficult conversation, remind yourself to pause and think. You don't have to accept the invitation to enter every fight you are invited to, nor do you need to engage in every confrontation. If your spouse brings up something mean or nasty or unfair, don't allow yourself to jump into that battle. Be a person who thinks on good things, and you will be less likely to respond negatively. At some point, your positive attitude and approach to difficult situations can produce hope in your spouse.

At another workshop, I shocked the participants when I said, "Keep in mind, there are no emergencies in your relationship."

A woman spoke up and said, "What do you mean? I feel like our marriage is in a state of emergency right now!"

I smiled and said, "No, you may have discovered something painful, hurtful, traumatic, and possibly even life changing about your spouse or yourself, but it is not an emergency and will not normally cause you to die. Moreover, you are not going to fix that situation in a few minutes. Think about it: if you spent the past ten years messing up your marriage, it doesn't make sense to think you can recreate the marriage of your dreams within a few days or weeks. Making something more urgent than it actually is tends to allow your emotions to drive your response, but that will not positively influence your relationship. Even if you discovered yesterday that your spouse is having an affair, that did not happen overnight. It has been developing for some time, whether you were aware of it or not."

Since I had told our story at the workshop, I referred back to our experience.

"When I looked at Shannon and said, 'I don't love you anymore,' she was shocked, but the actions and attitudes that had brought us to that juncture had not just happened. Those things had been happening for some time in our marriage. We were broken long before that, and we weren't going to be fixed instantly.

"When you obsess over the failing parts of your relationship, you can create problems that don't really exist. Remember: no matter how much you think you know about your marriage partner, there are some things you don't. And we aren't comfortable with those gaps. When we are in a negative emotional state, it is highly unlikely that we are going to fill that hole with positive information. Instead, we plug it with statements our friends may have told us, or movies or television shows about marital infidelities, or worse yet, fantasies and imaginations that exist only in our heads. These are self-imposed potholes you don't need to hit. Instead, win the battles in your mind by choosing to focus on the positive things you can do. To win the battle of the mind is crucial, and it is always a choice.

"Even small changes in your thoughts and attitude can make a major change. Find one thing that you can begin to work on in you. If you never are reconciled with your spouse, you will still be a better person. It is not easy to put yourself in a better place, but it might just change the remainder of your life and that of your spouse."

• • • • •

One of the key elements I emphasize in my marriage coaching practice is forgiveness—forgiving the person (or people) who hurt you and forgiving yourself for your part in the pain as well.

Certainly, seeking the forgiveness of God is a top priority, but even for people who don't believe in God, extending and receiving forgiveness is crucial. It's nearly impossible for a couple whose marriage is in trouble to be reconciled in any meaningful way if they refuse to deal with forgiveness. To be emotionally healthy, there can be no harboring of bitterness, resentment, and unforgiveness. "Forgiveness is the heart of the matter," as songwriter and founding member of the Eagles, Don Henley, reminded us, "even if you don't love me anymore."

CHAPTER 35

THE HERO IS SHANNON

Shannon started forgiving me for my indiscretions almost immediately after she discovered them. She not only said the words "I forgive you," she demonstrated them on a daily basis. She is the kindest and most forgiving person I have ever known. Moreover, she refused to give up on me. She continued to pray for me, but to her surprise, God answered one of her prayers with a rebuke. She remembers, "Before we got back together, I was praying for God to change Jimmy, believing that He could supernaturally turn him around and *make* him do what was right. But God showed me, 'I'm not going to make Jimmy love you. You must surrender him.' I wanted to argue with God and quote verses of Scripture about persevering in prayer, but the Lord showed me that I had to take my hands off the situation. It was hard, but I finally acquiesced."

She surrendered our marriage. She forgave me. She didn't give up on us, nor did she ever stop believing in us and that we could be reconciled. But she surrendered *me* and surrendered her trying to influence me. Interestingly, God did, indeed, turn me around.

Shannon's ability to remain strong still amazes me. I cannot fathom the mental and emotional anguish I caused her, yet she endured. Nor did I, or do I, deserve the way she so graciously dealt with my insolent folly. She is not a boisterous person or one to stand up on a rock and preach to others. But she modeled true Christianity in the way she continued to trust God; she believed when He told her, "Be still and know that I am God," that He had her best interests at heart. She continued to love me unconditionally. She was not absent of fear, but she courageously believed and hoped for the best, despite her worst fears that our marriage might dissolve in divorce.

She also worked hard to better herself, strengthening her PIES, the physical, intellectual, emotional, and spiritual aspects of her life. Shannon recalls, "Instead of wallowing in 'Woe is me,' I decided, 'I am going to take authority over my own life.' When you are in the middle of the storm, you might as well learn something from it."

Long before Shannon and I attended the Marriage Helper workshop, and then later were reconciled, Shannon had already begun working on her PIES. We later learned how important these things were, but at the time, we didn't know anything about the PIES. Yet almost instinctively, or perhaps it was the Spirit of God guiding her, Shannon began working on the physical, intellectual, emotional, and spiritual aspects of her life. While my life, self-esteem, and faith were still in shambles, Shannon's were on the rise. Instead of whining about how much she didn't like the situation, Shannon grew through the mess.

Consequently, when we got back together, I was still a basket case, but Shannon was a big part of my healing since she had already begun the healing process for herself. Moreover, she was totally different from the person I had left, because she had made progress in her physical appearance, in her confidence, and in her faith.

Despite the fresh start in our marriage, when we got back together, it was not as if we stepped into some sort of fairy-tale existence, where everything is beautiful and everyone lives happily ever after. No, since our reconciliation, Shannon and I have continued to work through many of our own struggles. We've still had days when we returned to bad habits, but now we have the emotional tools to cope with those. We practiced the things we learned about how to improve our own relationship.

Shannon says, "Looking back, I now realize how much I didn't know about my husband, what he needed, and how he responded. In many ways, our early marriage was so superficial.

"And some of those habits were hard to break. I'm thankful for the marriage we have now because when one or both of us falls back, we can help each other, because we now have a better, deeper knowledge of ourselves and how we can help each other."

Dealing with my depression, anxiety, and panic syndrome was a major new experience for both of us. Prior to the affair, we did not realize that there were actually physiological occurrences in my body and brain that could profoundly influence my actions and attitudes. While I had experienced emotional "downers" previously, we knew now that there were medical reasons for my feelings of depression as well.

Shannon continued working on herself, trying to develop a more positive mindset, so she did not always know how to deal with my depression. Certain times of year triggered memories or feelings that tugged at her heart. Other situations also caused her concerns. At first, she perceived some of my morose expressions as possibly being the result of having another affair. I wasn't, but we were both learning how to understand my slumps. To this day, if I don't take my medication, Shannon may find me in tears. We continue to work together, relearning how to live together in love.

• • • • •

Almost every week I encounter people who have gotten caught up in affairs or are living in limerence, hoping their fantasies will come true. Many of them have walked away from all that is stable and good in their lives, willing to give up everything they have always cherished for a fanciful chance to be with their fantasy lover.

During one marriage workshop in which I was involved, a female Sunday school teacher was particularly adamant about her desire to leave her husband and children the following week and move in with her drug-addicted lover. A group of well-intentioned women at the event cornered her and said, "Listen, if God came down here right now and told you that He was going to take one of your children if you don't change your mind, what would you say?"

The woman in limerence looked back at the women and callously replied, "I'd tell Him to choose which one He wants."

The delusion of limerence and the power of the state of mind it produces is devilishly destructive.

Sad to say, I've heard and witnessed countless similar comments, attitudes, and actions. But before I get up on a soapbox and start thinking in condescending terms toward anyone else, I remind myself that, at one season in my life, I, too, was not far from that mindset.

Many spouses give up hoping for reconciliation at that point. "I'm done. I can't take it anymore," he or she might say. "I quit. Go do what you want to do."

But today, I look back at them and say, "Everyone with whom I speak about these matters says that at some point. But please, don't give up. There really is hope."

At nearly every workshop or conference at which I speak, I tell our story, not simply to evoke pity or to toot our own horn but to give other couples hope that regardless of how far gone they feel their marriage is, they can still recover and rebuild. Many clients that come to me say, "I think we are the exception; we're too far gone."

I tell them some of the things that Shannon and I experienced. Then I tell them, "This stuff works."

Many of those relationships have been saved, but it doesn't happen by accident.

Because of my direct manner, sometimes I shock people when I say, "You've done what you needed to do to get you right where you are today. You think this situation 'just happened,' but it didn't. It was a direct result of what you put your hands, feet, mind, and energy toward in the months and possibly years prior to this. The good news is this: You can start to do something different at any time. You can start doing the right things today, right now."

Forgiveness is a major key to moving forward, whether you are reunited with your spouse or not.

One day in the early stages of our reconciliation, Shannon and I were sitting in the car outside the office of a veterinarian where she had taken our beloved dog, Max. We love dogs, and we were both distraught because it seemed certain that Max was not going to be with us much longer. Since I had left Shannon, Max had been her best friend, her companion, through all the transitions she had experienced.

"I'm sorry for all that I have said and done to hurt you," I told Shannon. "Would you please forgive me?"

I knew that Shannon had forgiven me in her heart a long time ago, yet it was still important for me to seek her forgiveness, as well as God's forgiveness, and to muster the will to forgive myself.

Although there was no direct link between me having an affair and the church in Trumbull, I also felt it was important for me to forgive my church family in Connecticut, specifically our two close friends, Micah and Charlotte, who had felt like family to me yet had traveled four hours to denigrate my sixteen-year ministry with them and disparage my ministry potential for anyone else. I've never understood the motives for their actions, but I knew I could no longer hold animosity toward them. Regardless of their reasons, no doubt, they felt compelled to speak up, and they did what they felt right about doing, even if it turned out to be malicious. Still, I had allowed resentment to seethe in my spirit for far too long, and I had to come to grips with that. I didn't want to let it live another moment. I still loved the church and the people, and to this day the pastors and congregation are doing a great work there. The people of the congregation were like a family to Shannon and me, and I wished them well. Most of the people with whom we had spent sixteen years of our lives had no idea what had happened or why we never returned to visit. Nor did I ever tell them, until now. But the most important part of the past, for me, was forgiving the people who had attempted to hurt me. It took time, and it wasn't easy. The residual pain stayed with me a long time. But it was important that I, who had been forgiven much, should also forgive much.

Following the affair with Vanessa, I had friends say, "Why didn't you talk to me? I would have understood. I'd have prayed with you or tried to help somehow. Why didn't you say that you were hurting because of what your friends had done or tell us about the discontent in your marriage?"

"Because you would have betrayed me," I said, reflecting some of the residual effect of what my spiritual friends had done to me. Because of their actions, I no longer trusted anyone.

But when I learned how to forgive, I found true freedom. I am still learning, and there are times when I have to remind myself that because God forgives me and Shannon forgives me, I can forgive the people who have hurt me.

Interestingly, Tim Moen, the pastor who had the unenviable responsibility of picking up the pieces of the mess I left in

Massachusetts, extended an invitation for me to return to the church as a guest speaker. Tim was another person I thought I couldn't trust, but he proved me wrong. He stuck with me through all of my foolishness and continued to believe in me and encourage me. He was a true friend to me and proved that it is possible to rebuild trust and experience forgiveness and restoration, no matter what a person has done.

Tim is a marvelous example of God's unconditional love. Perhaps because of his influence, one aspect of coaching that I hope to continue is helping pastors who have experienced a moral failure in their ministry. For so many of them, there is nobody to whom they can speak honestly without fear of reprisal or loss of confidentiality. Perhaps that is why so few pastors who mess up ever return to a viable ministry. Instead, they leave the ministry and live with a sense of perpetual disqualification. They settle for working in a career to which they were not called and in which they find little fulfillment or contentment; all the while, the gifts and callings of God on their lives are irrevocable.

Pourteau Coaching, our new organization, focuses on developing or rebuilding a positive mindset. We emphasize keys to restoration, presenting a pathway for executives, high-profile public figures, and especially ministers to return to usefulness in their giftings.

Marriage Helper rescues people who are near the end of their rope regarding their relationships. Most of the couples are at odds with each other and hanging on by a thread when they walk into our workshops. I'm glad to help deal with the crisis marriages, but I am also intent on helping everyday people safeguard and strengthen their marriages *before* they get into trouble. I want to focus more on prevention, enrichment, and creating a mindset of daily positivity. I want to help people struggling with more complex issues as well.

For some reason, God has given me favor with helping high-profile celebrities and newsmakers who are trying to strengthen or rebuild their marriages. Regardless of a person's prestige, power, or financial resources, people are not all that different. We have the same basic needs; we crave the same sort of things, although we may look for those things in different manners or through different means. Through Pourteau Coaching, I want to help people who are not currently being reached. Many of those are not down-and-outers; surprisingly, they are "up-and-outers."

I still enjoy speaking in front of large groups of people, using my humor to zip in some zingers that will have an impact. Dr. Joe Beam described our differing approaches yet tandem presentations. "I'm more the academic, the teacher, presenting information that will help a person long-term," Joe says, "and you are more of the motivator-evangelist type, spreading layers of truth and firing quick, hard-hitting nuggets that people can grab on to and put to use in their lives immediately."

I think Joe is right.

I want to be a dealer of hope. Shannon and I have learned some lessons the hard way, and we want to help as many people as we can to avoid the pitfalls we experienced. We are not the "poster kids" for how to have a good marriage, nor do we want to be. Rather, we are a day-to-day living example of what hope can do despite bad decisions and in the midst of life's worst trials.

· · · · ·

What can you do right now if your marriage is struggling or even in deep trouble? Perhaps you or your spouse are embroiled in an affair and one or both of you wants to end the marriage or wonders if it is worth it to attempt to save it. Or maybe you are trying to help someone else save a marriage. What do you need to know?

Believe that there is hope. You are not alone in your experience; others have been where you are and have come through to a new and better marriage relationship. That is what happened for Shannon and me. This can happen for you. Perhaps you should seek out a workshop such as Marriage Helper. But maybe you or your spouse are not ready for that yet. What do you do in the meantime?

Today and tomorrow and over the next few days, begin to change one thing about how you think or act. Just one. Start small; start with something achievable and build from there.

Live the best life you can right now. Live a life that brings energy and faith back into your heart and mind and improves the PIES in your life. Keep in mind that God may be using your experiences to build faith in you. I talked to a person who had been devastated by a spouse having an affair. "You do realize that God can use this time to build faith in you," I said.

"What are you talking about, Jim?" the person asked, aghast. "Are you saying my faith can be stronger in the middle of all this?"

"No, your faith will be stronger *because* of all this," I replied. "When you're living on a spiritual mountaintop, you don't need extra faith in God, but when you are going through those valleys, when all hell is breaking loose in your life, He often uses those experiences to strengthen your faith and give you hope."

There is hope, no matter what you feel at this moment. Hope is not a guarantee; it is not absolute assurance. Hope is potential. You have the potential to make your marriage work better. If you will take your thoughts captive and keep them in the realm of the positive, you can affect your own actions and be in a better place to influence your relationship with your spouse.

Simply put, focus on what you want rather than what you don't want to happen. If you look with tunnel vision on what you fear, life becomes a self-fulfilling prophecy, and those things you fear will come to pass in your experience.

I love to ride motorcycles. One of the most important principles in safely operating a motorcycle is to look where you want to go, not at the cars or other obstacles around you. Some of the most common accidents that motorcycle riders have—hitting guardrails and other objects—are the result of focusing on the obstacle rather than on the road ahead. The cyclists see themselves getting close to something that is dangerous—an accident waiting to happen— and they focus on what they don't want to hit. Inevitably, they are drawn toward the obstacle. They run into what they don't want to because that is what they have focused on.

The same thing often happens in relationships. So focus on what you want rather than what you don't want. Speak the truth you want to see in your life and relationship. Think on those things and act on them. If you are a person of faith, focus on the truth that God is for your marriage, that He wants you to succeed, and, that He will do His part in helping you if you will do yours.

Regardless of how bad your circumstances might seem, you still have the choice to do what you need to do based on your values. You can do the right things and live free of guilt, staying focused on what you want.

What do you have to lose? You can be miserable if you allow yourself. But if you will step out in faith, who knows where you will land?

The African impala is a small, deer-like animal that lives in the wilderness plains adjacent to the jungle. It has the ability to leap ten feet high, and with a running start at full stride it can cover a distance of nearly thirty feet.

How can this amazing animal be held captive?

Trainers discovered that all they had to do to constrain the impala was build a three-foot-high wall around the perimeter of the property. Because of past experiences, the impala will not attempt to leap over the wall unless it can see where its feet will land. The impala may run and jump with all of its friends within the perimeter, but when it approaches the wall, it will stop and shy away. It forgets all the greatness it has within and only considers the obstacle. Because it can't see the ending, it refuses to jump.

Many people who want to see a marriage improved are similar to that impala. They have incredible potential to create the marriage they want, the family they have always dreamed of, and the lifestyle they desire. But they refuse to take that leap of faith because they are afraid or uncertain where they might land.

Yes, it takes faith to leap when you cannot see what lies ahead. It may seem like a colossal risk, but it is not blind faith or an uncalculated risk. You have the potential to make your marriage work. Always remember: no matter what you have done or what you have endured, even after an affair, hope is where the heart is. Your past need not define your future. You can dare to leap!

The question is, Are you ready?

TO CONTACT JIM POURTEAU COACHING,
VISIT JIMPOURTEAU.COM